THE SOUTHERN EYE

Yousif M. Qasmiyeh is a Palestinian scholar and poet who was born and educated in Baddawi refugee camp and whose doctoral research at the University of Oxford examined containment and the archive in 'refugee writing.' His poetry and prose have appeared in journals including *MPT*, *Stand*, *PN Review* and *Poetry London*. His collection, *Writing the Camp* (Broken Sleep Books, 2021) was a Poetry Book Society Recommendation, and was shortlisted for the Royal Society of Literature's Ondaatje Prize. His latest book is *Eating the Archive* (2023, Broken Sleep Books).

Elena Fiddian-Qasmiyeh is Professor in Migration and Refugee Studies at UCL where she co-directs the Migration Research Unit. She is Principal Investigator of *Refugee Hosts* and *Southern Responses to Displacement,* and Joint-Lead (with Yousif M. Qasmiyeh) of the *Baddawi Camp Research Lab*. Her books include *The Ideal Refugees*; *South-South Educational Migration, Humanitarianism and Development*; *The Oxford Handbook of Refugee and Forced Migration Studies*; *The Handbook of South-South Relations*; *The Oxford Handbook of Religion and Contemporary Migration*; and *Refuge in a Moving World.*

Saiful Huq Omi is a critically acclaimed photographer, filmmaker, educator, and activist. His photography, films and writing focus on human rights, politics of identity, and displacement. He has published over half a dozen books and has been working on and archiving the Rohingya crisis through photography for over a decade. In 2012, he founded *Counter Foto - A Centre for Visual Arts* in Dhaka, Bangladesh, which provides world-class photography education with a specialization in human rights and social justice.

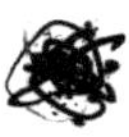

ISBN: 978-1-916938-42-7

Cover designed by Aaron Kent

Edited and Typeset by Aaron Kent

Broken Sleep Books Ltd
PO BOX 102
Llandysul
SA44 9BG

The Southern Eye: Co-Seeing Displacements

Yousif M. Qasmiyeh
Elena Fiddian-Qasmiyeh
Saiful Huq Omi

Broken Sleep Books

CONTENTS

PRAISE for *The Southern Eye*

Revisiting this book is far from nostalgia's predictability. It is possible that everyone in these pictures, and the objects, and the scenery, might already, or soon, be wiped out. Yet, crucially, this book is part of the strong continuity that arises from imaginative co-creation and co-curation. The South-South gaze, between Rohingya and Palestinian, brilliantly undoes the traps and theories of photography as the record of an instant, a snap, a capture, or a document. Here is the grain of activity in the camp. The accompanying text weaves images into stories, making each scene an archive of the past and the future: the kind of past that might have kept happening, the kind of future that could be. Together, word and image extend life beyond the frame. The frame is there to invite us to think beyond limits and parallels. The Southern Eye makes me want to look again and again. Like rain into the veins of the earth, it feeds and waters an intimate vision of our world repeatedly being made possible.

— Anthony Vahni Capildeo

This volume is a beautiful experiment in poetic/pictorial juxtaposition. Comprising extended prose poems and short essays alongside assorted photographs – archival, authorial and amateur – it explores the refugee situation as mediated via text and image while positing South/South synergies and connections. Whether recycled from albums or personal archives, or produced on site and location, this collection of extraordinary and ordinary pictures invokes life-worlds and livings that are both precarious and precious. The carefully crafted words that accompany them constitute a suggestive and extended frame for thinking. They are neither prescriptive nor didactic. They hold, like the photographs themselves, an infinite and exquisite set of possibilities.

— Tamar Garb

The Southern Eye: a collection of photographs and poems moving between the everyday, the urgent and the emergency, fortified by a poetic that is at once as striking as it is necessary.

— Anthony Anaxagorou

Built on a series of encounters between image and text, this unique book compels readers to see both photography and prose in a new light. As you look and read, each image becomes a stanza, whilst words become lenses that refocus our gaze. Interrogating the conditions of seeing and being seen with the warmth of a documentary and the force of a vision, this volume is as intimate as it is resonant, as stirring as it is revealing.

— Daniele Rugo

them to the white plastic inside the album. That was the album that was taken with us, as a memento of our presence, the one dictated by air raids, wars and gunshots. He would always say: *Do we have everything?* And by everything he meant everything of relevance to those forced disappearances. The album was also an amulet. A holy text to quench our thirst and sight in time of need.

We remember in photography so our hearts and minds might be lighter one day.

The click is a heartbeat that long escaped from our tired hearts.

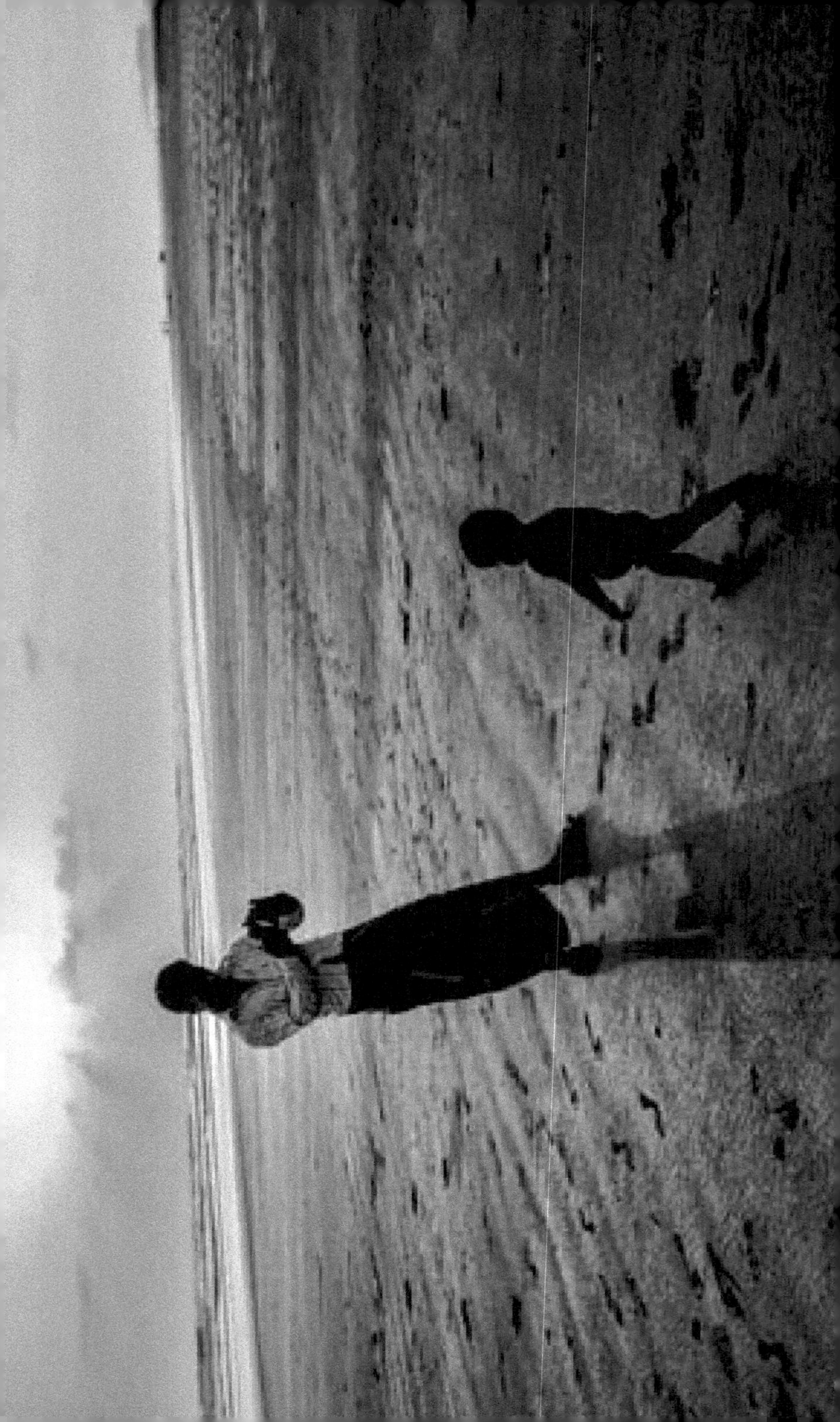

IN OTHER EYES, THE ARCHIVE HAPPENS

In his image, all is created. This is the arch-creator worshipping his image by seeing it as the only rightful heir of the face. In the photograph before us, creation is carved from within, meticulously molded into multiplicity: the man photographs the child and the photographer photographs both the photographer and the photographed to archive photography, alongside the preceding eyes, as distinct times. Before I enter the photograph, I wait on the edge, to borrow some time from this endlessness. There are disparate footprints, traces of the man and the child, and of those who preceded them or have just passed. The camera, inside the photograph, is pointing slightly downwards to match the child's height and capture his small stature as he treads along. It is a jovial view and yet appears to quickly transition into a dead end even though they are still somewhere in the middle. It is a photograph-narrative, a throbbing memory, coupled with the sudden realisation that those inside will unknowingly venture into the outside world, thinking that living, in this instance, outside the photograph, always happens in the aftermath of a photograph.

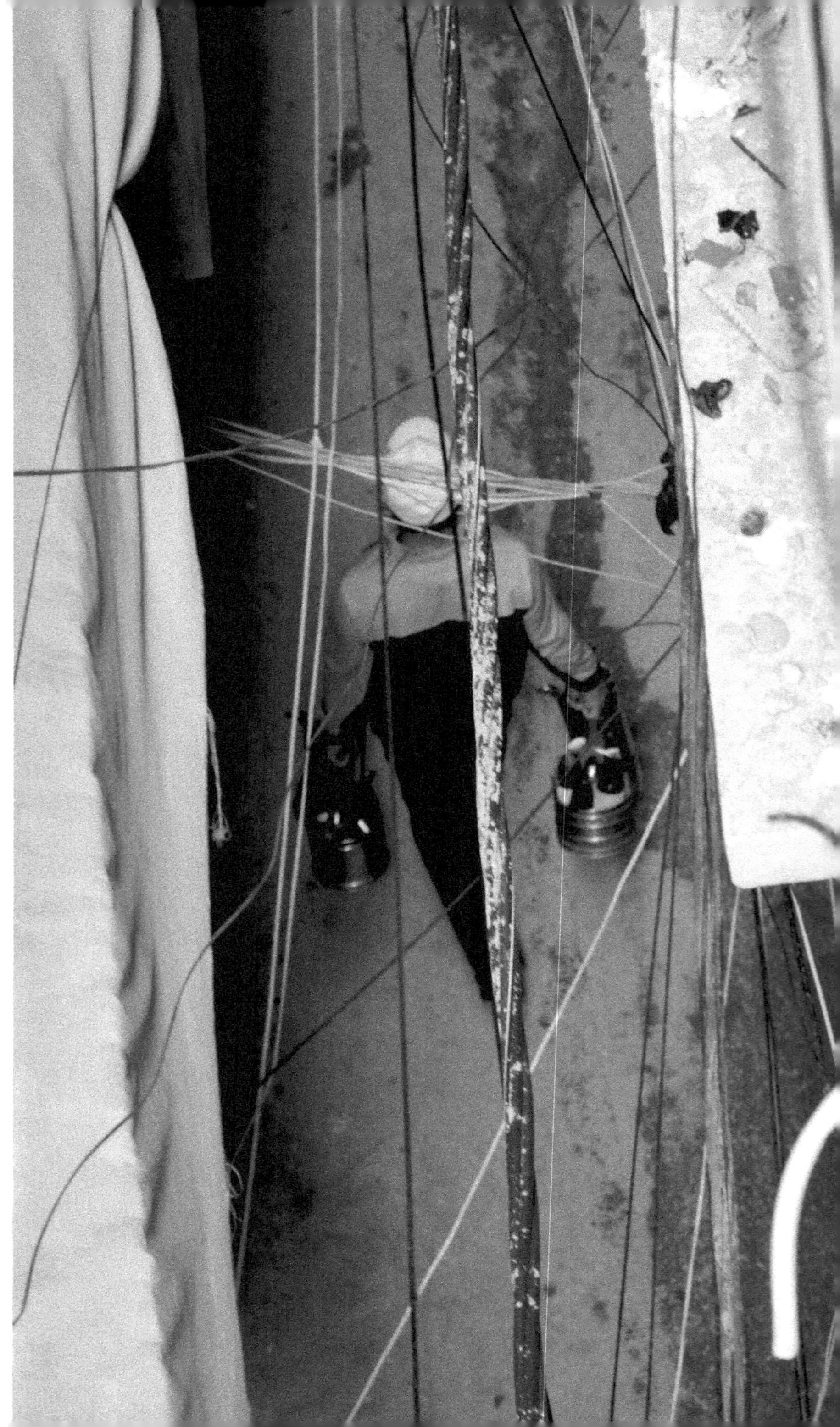

THERE WILL ALWAYS BE A VENDOR BEFORE AND AFTER THE PICTURE

It is a photograph of a coffee vendor in motion; of somebody who is familiar enough with the routes of the camp to roam them with relative ease.

The clanking of the cups, emanating from the collision of two porcelain cups – fragile but not too fragile – in the vendor's hand, can still be heard or seen from beyond the picture.

But what is the clanking for? What does it signify amongst other signifiers, in a noisy context such as the camp where sounds continually fight for a space to be(come) sounds.

The truly inaudible clanking is nothing but a testimony of arrival into a place, a shibboleth, a different dialect.

The vendor will soon escape the picture or be pushed away by another.

However, somewhere, there will always be a vendor before or after the picture, or more precisely inside of it, boiling his coffee in silence.

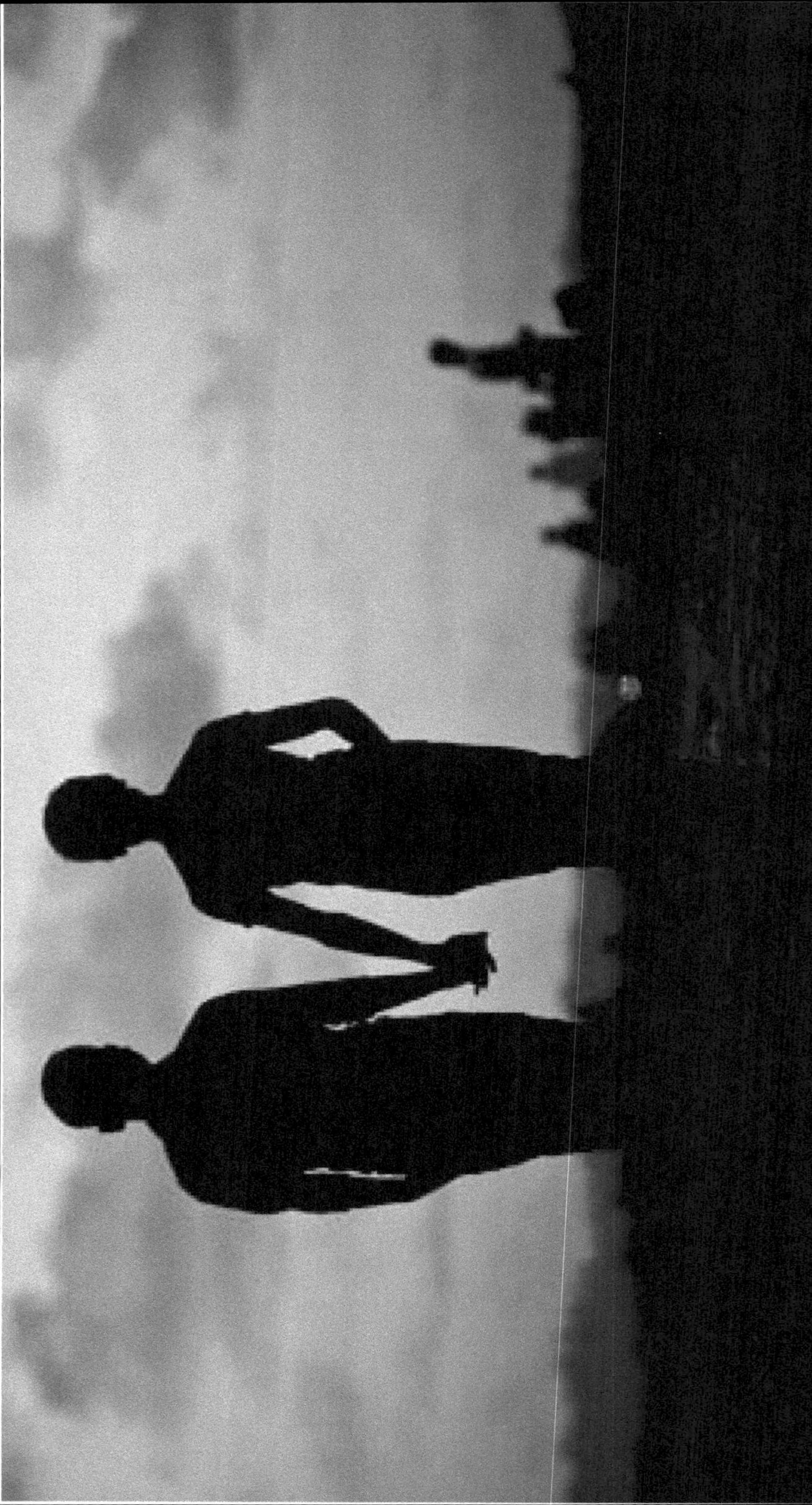

THE DUAL

Togetherness usually excepts the dual, thus rendering it neither entirely singular nor plural but a mercenary of its own state. Through the photograph, the body is transposed to other bodies embracing, holding hands or walking in sync to somewhere, to bodies that, even when alone, exist in-relation. Sheltered by the sky, two bodies are walking away, hands locked, in intimacy and friendship, as though it is more their common destiny than a mundane outing. While the faces are physically near, they are facing the other way, withholding themselves from any excess exposure. It is a walk in the direction of dispersed silhouettes of people, still figures of different sizes, towards a stage set for the imminent entry of the dual.

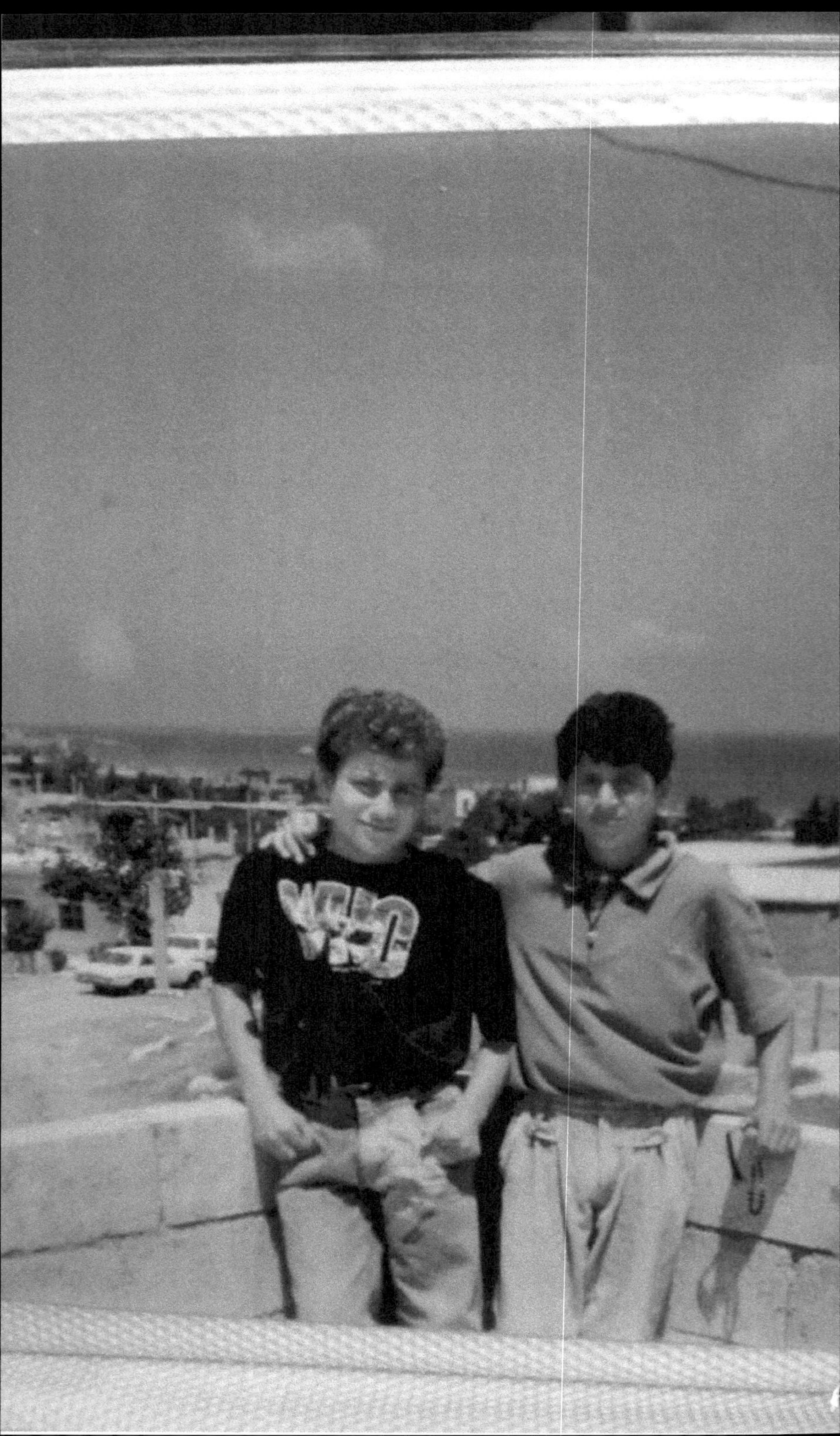

IN THAT TIME

With their fingertips, in their family archive, they dug deep to come back with a photograph of two boys: their son and his friend. The son, as shared by the older brother, is the one wrapping his arm around his friend. The sky looks clear and vast and is tenderly caressed by the sea at the bottom. The two boys already look in post-the-photograph mood, in the exact time that shepherds the past and the present into some kind of a future. Stuck in an album one time and unstuck to make access easier, the photograph is manhandled, held and put down many times, to see if more could be seen. Old conversations are revisited in the present whispers as to what it was that the photograph tried to capture. Was it to preserve an instant, an innocent instant, on its way to dissolution? Or was it a testament to the changing character of what surrounds the camp of places and people? That was the stretch of land which, for us, was as near to the camp as it was far from it – a place where photographs were taken regularly for the mere reason: *Out there* is another presence.

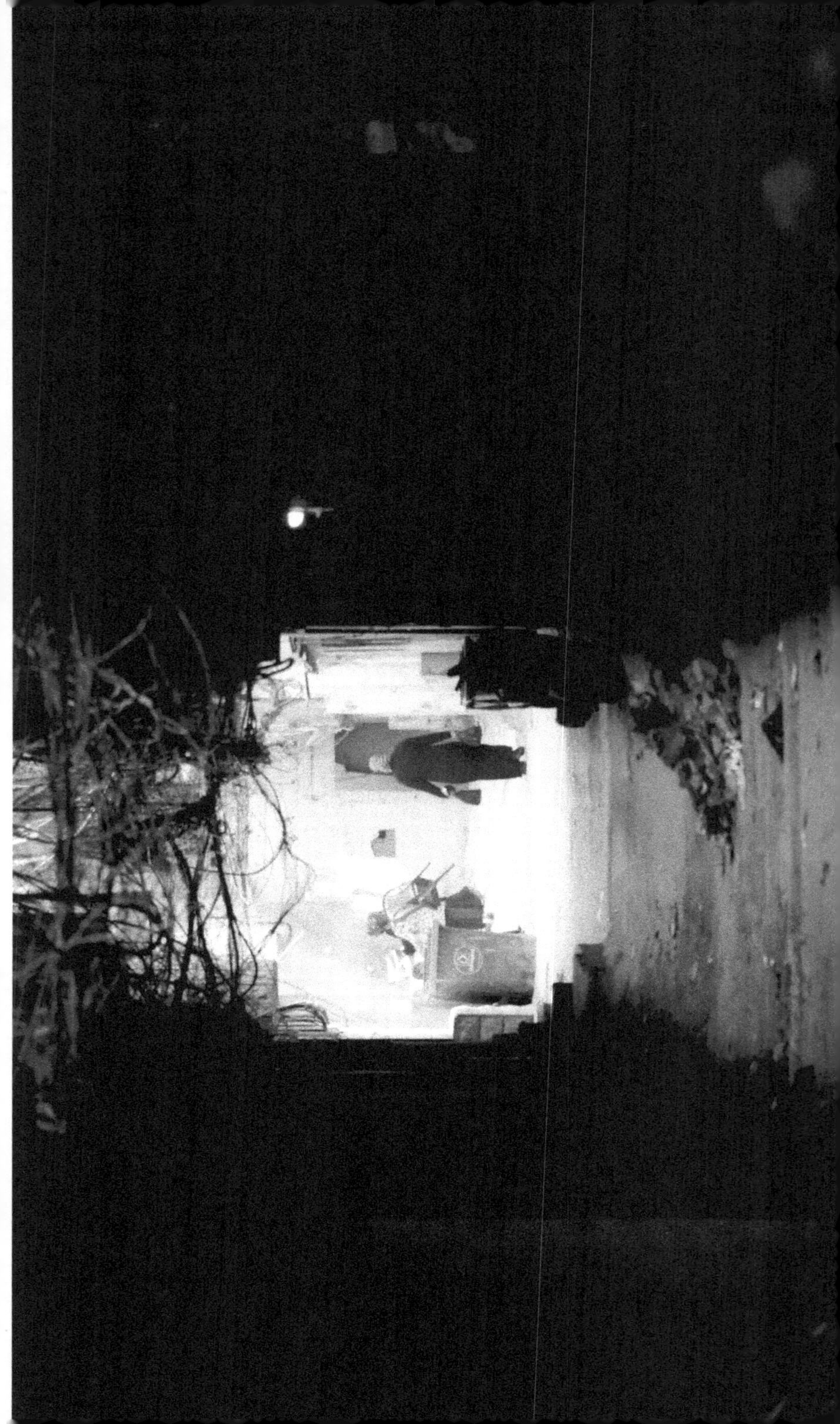

EXISTING IN ANTICIPATION

Details are for those in a hurry not the seer. Seeing engenders its own details – details that seem to happen in the folds of the seen with minimal reverting to what comes before and after the photograph. The photograph moves towards light, from a tunnel-like state to a quasi-resolution that is cut short by the wall of a house at the far end. This is the rite of passage, ours, to corners concerned above all else with the very meaning of living as a pact with memory. The hanging cables act as an arbour of some sort, a material shading in the absence of a sky that is lost on its way to the camp while the ground offers a path that appears well-trodden and distant at the same time. Bins, green in colour, placed on each side of the alley with differing visibility, echoing the green door towards which the woman in black slowly moves, all preceded by a mound of rubble and disparate and barely visible doorsteps. As we glimpse the woman in motion, balancing a shopping bag in each hand, veiled and draped in an abaya, the physical end of the photograph gradually intersects with the beginning of the woman's anticipated disappearance. Three figures to her left, one poking out, two standing, one holding a brown plastic chair as though gesturing towards the end of a time spent outside or the initiation of a new one. While this is part of an alley in Baddawi camp, it emulates other places where entering and exiting a place is on a par with sparing a moment to count your limbs, to check they are still with you. The woman could be my sister. Or a neighbour growing into distance to approximate her shadow. This is definitely walking in the footsteps of a time that is far away.

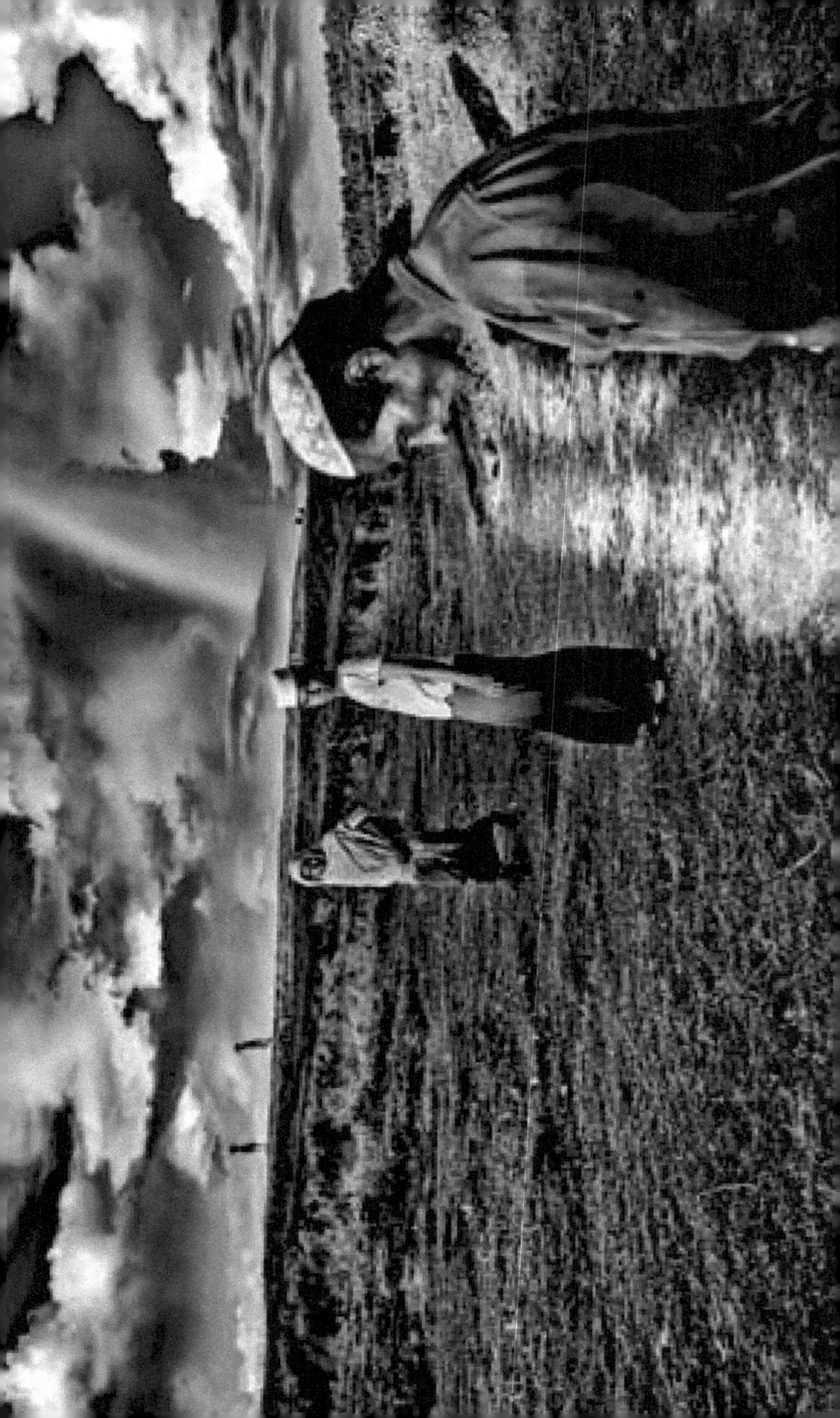

THE WAIT

Photographs can speak. Even though we articulate their silence in writing, we still cannot escape their intrinsic loudness. Everything looks ominous in this photograph: the path, the three main figures, and the sky. Surveying the edges, aridity seems to engulf and trap all. The older man's posture is between standing and kneeling; in a way, retaining its own liminality, the young boy, in the middle, is watching over, assiduously looking in the man's direction, while the older woman is at the other end, seeming to move closer, not away. In the distance, two stickman-like figures appear to be in deep conversation with the divine. The sky with its dense and weighty clouds seems to cave in on the entire scene. No one knows for certain what is about to happen and yet there is a sense of trepidation – we, as seers, co-wait, alongside those inside the photograph, anticipating with them without being involved in their destinies. In our presence, or absence, the man might cross the well-trodden path, or he might not – this is waiting not wanting to disclose its wait*ers*.

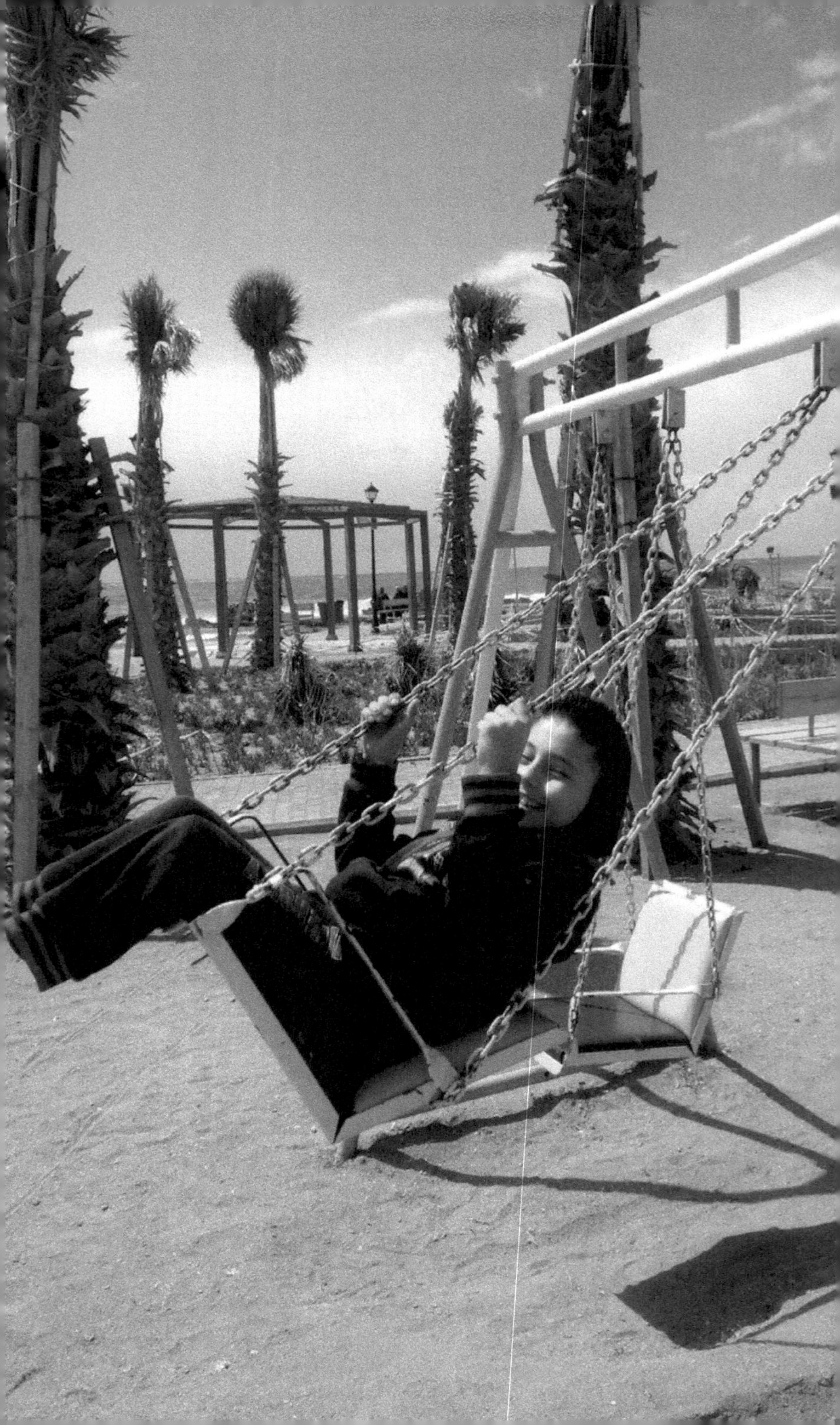

ON A SWING LIKE A ROCKING HEAVEN

To smile is to imagine arriving in a place with the barest of noises. This is why the intangibility in smiling is effectively harboured in the assumed silence of photography: The smile that is conveyed in the photograph is happening *now*. In this now, archived in the progressive, is a future. Zoom in and you shall see the absent legs flying in the air as organs without their body or as a mutilated body without its organs. We catch our breath as we look, trying to feed on the suspended in time. From Syria to Lebanon, bodies migrated, forced to distantiation, at times leaving themselves behind in haste. Exactly up high, on the swing, is where the boy's time is prolonged indefinitely, so much so that surviving as other is grasped in the incessant alteration between stillness and motion. The swing is being pushed, with force perhaps. From one side to another, departing and returning again. But who is it that caught such a pulse in the photograph? Who is it that caught it at such close range with the precision of a sniper? In a single night, on the back of an equine, the Prophet ascended into heaven; the boy, in history's face, smiles. Eyes shut but not blind, in serenity, pondering when the scarcity of remembrance might come.

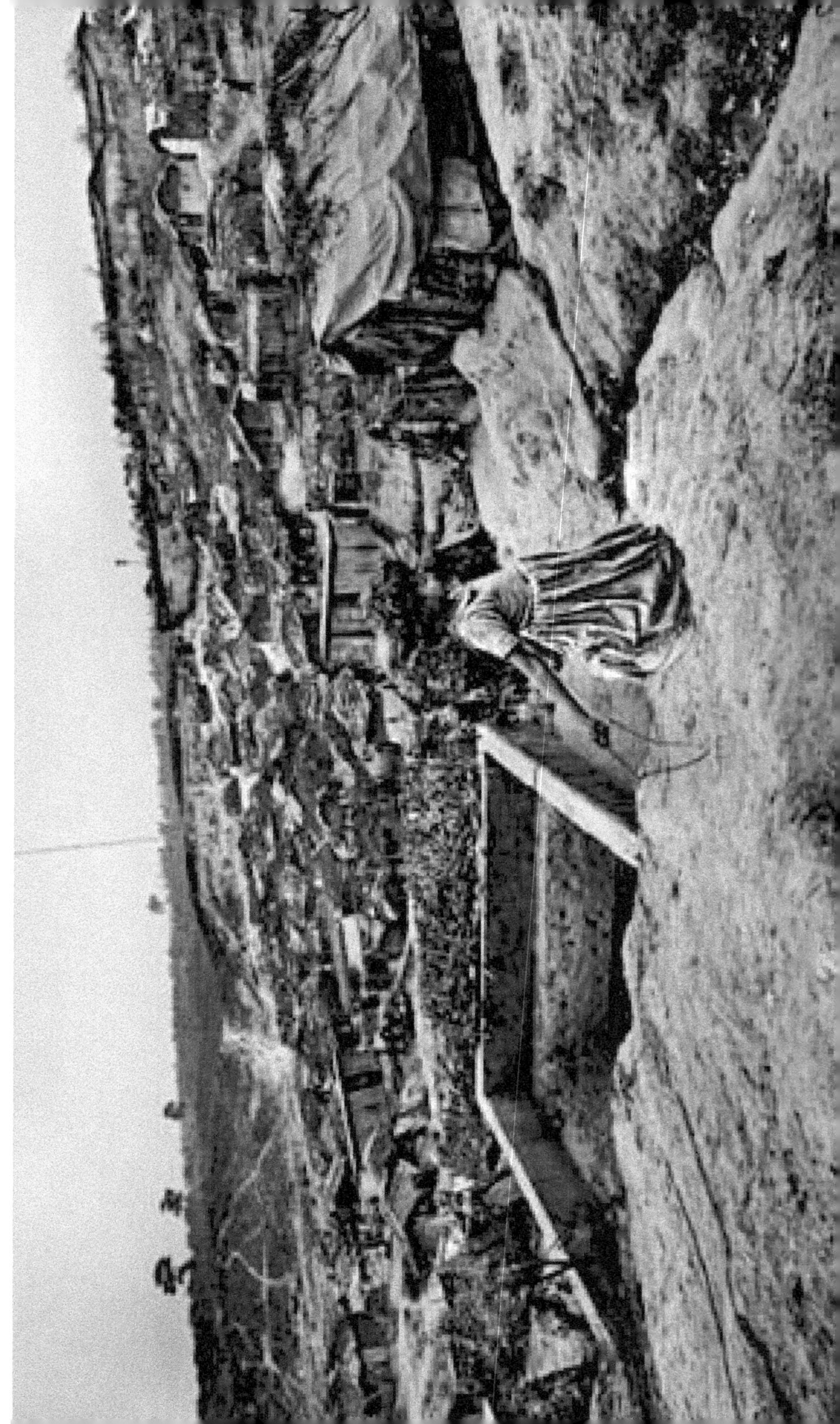

SKIPPING TOWARDS AN OUTSIDE

On a slightly elevated tip of what could be a makeshift refugee camp, a little girl is skipping. She is doing so alone. At first glance, neither her face nor the rope is discernible to the untrained eye, but as time passes, the girl's presence becomes more present. Her floating dress looks crumpled while suspended mid-air, enlarging the distance between her body and the earth, and swallowing her legs completely. She is flying, taking off from a point that is both adjacent to and distant from the scattered dwellings. There is a sensing, a movement towards a presumed exterior. While the skipping continues, the lens is left behind – as though the fleetingness of that instant is no longer sufficiently attained in the photograph but is instead reassembled in the coming vanishing of the girl.

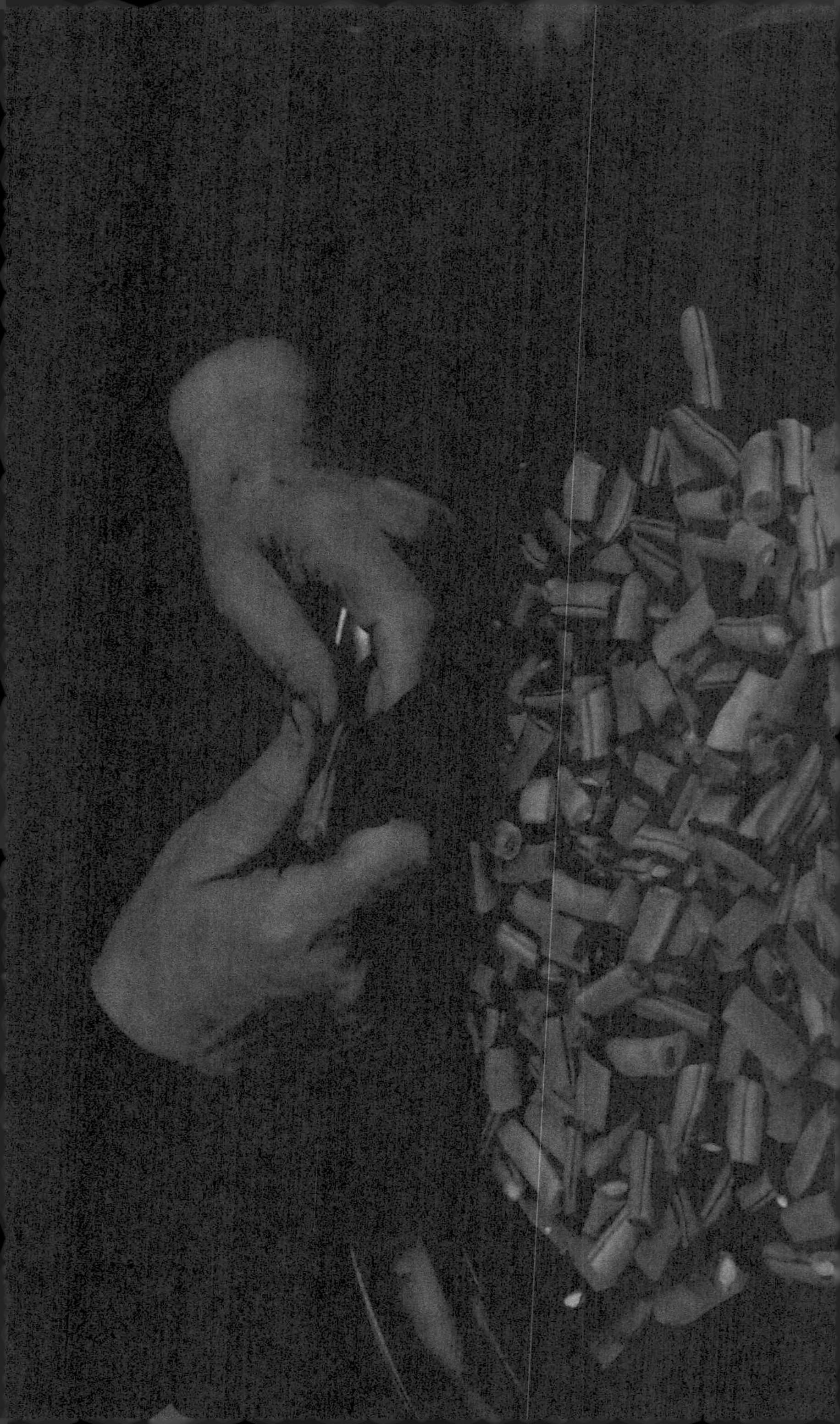

THE HANDS ARE HERS

The hands are hers – fractured urns of intimacy and anticipation.

They would cut, mend, darn, comb, bathe, clean, feel and above all submit themselves as seals of presence at the UNRWA distribution centres.

In this photograph, the face is outside the frame but the hands are certainly hers.

She is cutting runner beans, meticulously removing their fibrous ends and any impurities.

Her hands, the knife and the beans against the tin are the only elements in this landscape.

They all move in different directions and yet in total synchrony like a methodical machine.

The knife blade and the tin tray.

The hands and the beans.

The tray is the base, or more precisely the deathbed, for the fallen and everything perishable.

The hands are captured as close to and far from each other at the same time.

What is inextricable therein is sustained in the continuum of cutting, trimming and eventually the falling of the beans as singular and weakened parts.

The hands are certainly hers to the extent of complete dissolution and resurrection.

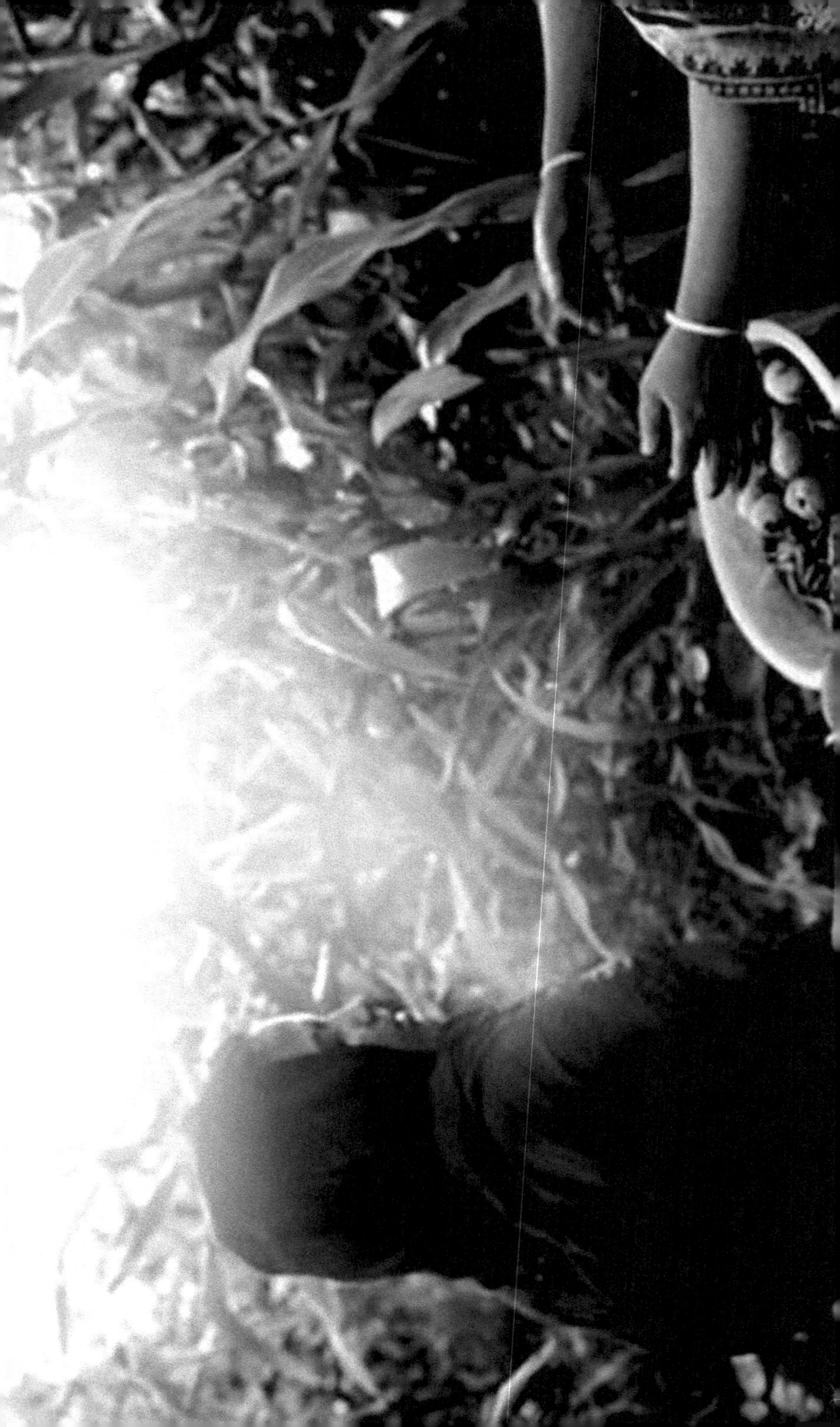

A BUCKET FULL OF LIGHT

When a photograph makes present, it subsequently makes absent. In this photograph, the bucket is shared between two people even though it is held by the one hand. There, produce is gathered, or at least is in the process of being gathered. The light of morning sunrays seems to radiate the upper part of the woman on the left, gently descending from afar while to the right, another person's hands – likely a woman's – are caught prior to or post an action. They are both in what could be a cornfield, either about to delve deeper into it or about to exit. Regardless, there is a halo awaiting the sacrificial in the coming crops.

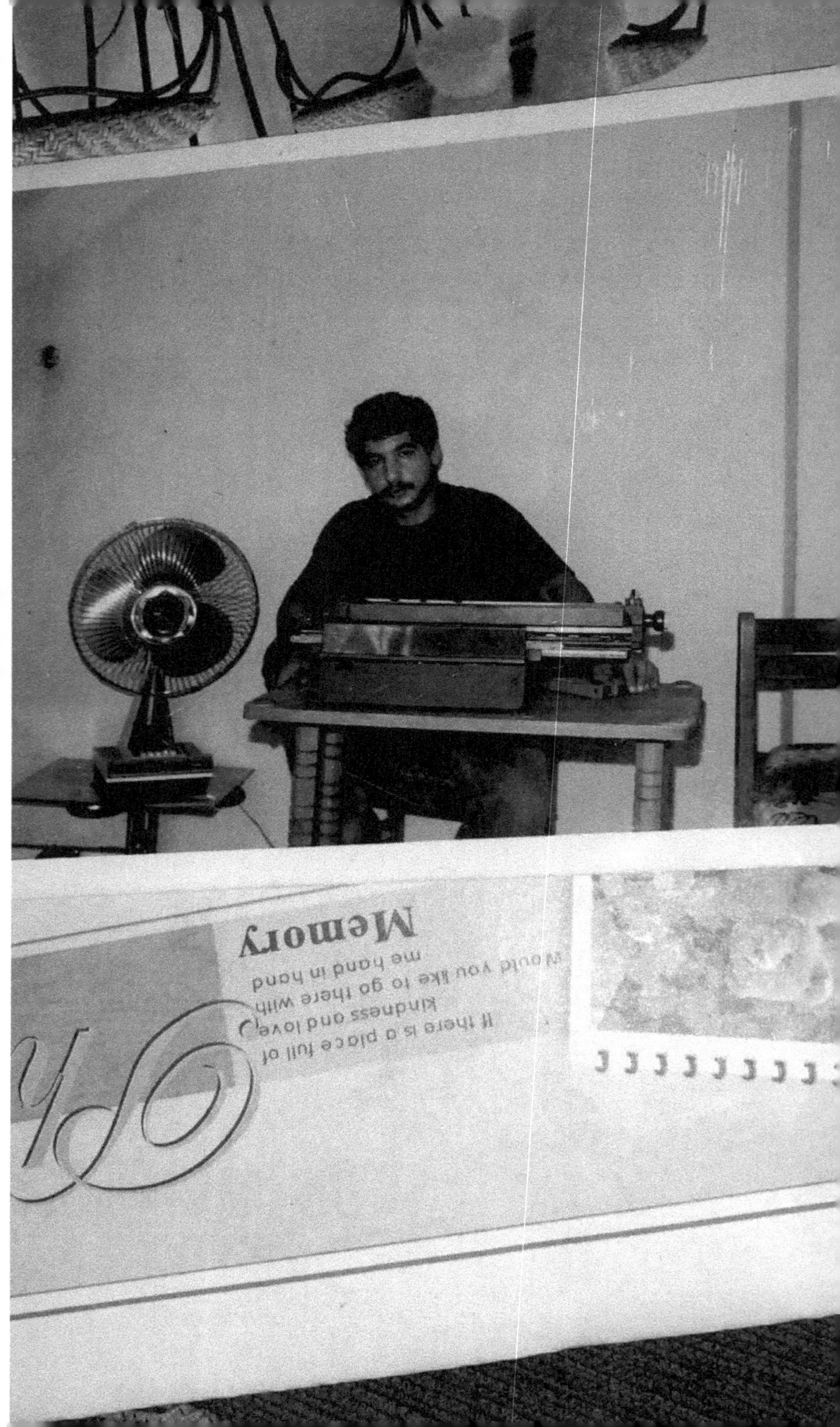
If there is a place full of
kindness and love
Would you like to go there with
me hand in hand
Memory

This is from the family album while pointing at a photograph of a man. "My father at work in Libya. Then they needed labour, and my father, alongside other Palestinian families, had wanted to leave the camp in search of a better life," the daughter confirmed. "This photograph was taken with the intention of sharing it with family members. It's a small gesture towards archiving that time and us," she continued.

As we look further, we see. Our eyes widen. We co-see, with the daughter's eyes, the father who is now a refugee in Norway with the rest of the family, the neutral look taking over from the entire body behind the wooden table. We look further, deeper into the face, into the father's presumed readiness for the click coming from the opposite side. We can see him at work, or where work was supposed to be undertaken. The fan to dampen the excruciating heat, the glass table to his side. There is also the word 'memory' outside the photograph, on the edge; what is integrally part of the album before becoming a home for memories. In this case, the English instead of the Arabic murmurs. Words float, from the daughter's mouth to our ears, we ask: "Why this one?". "This is more than a photograph," she answers.

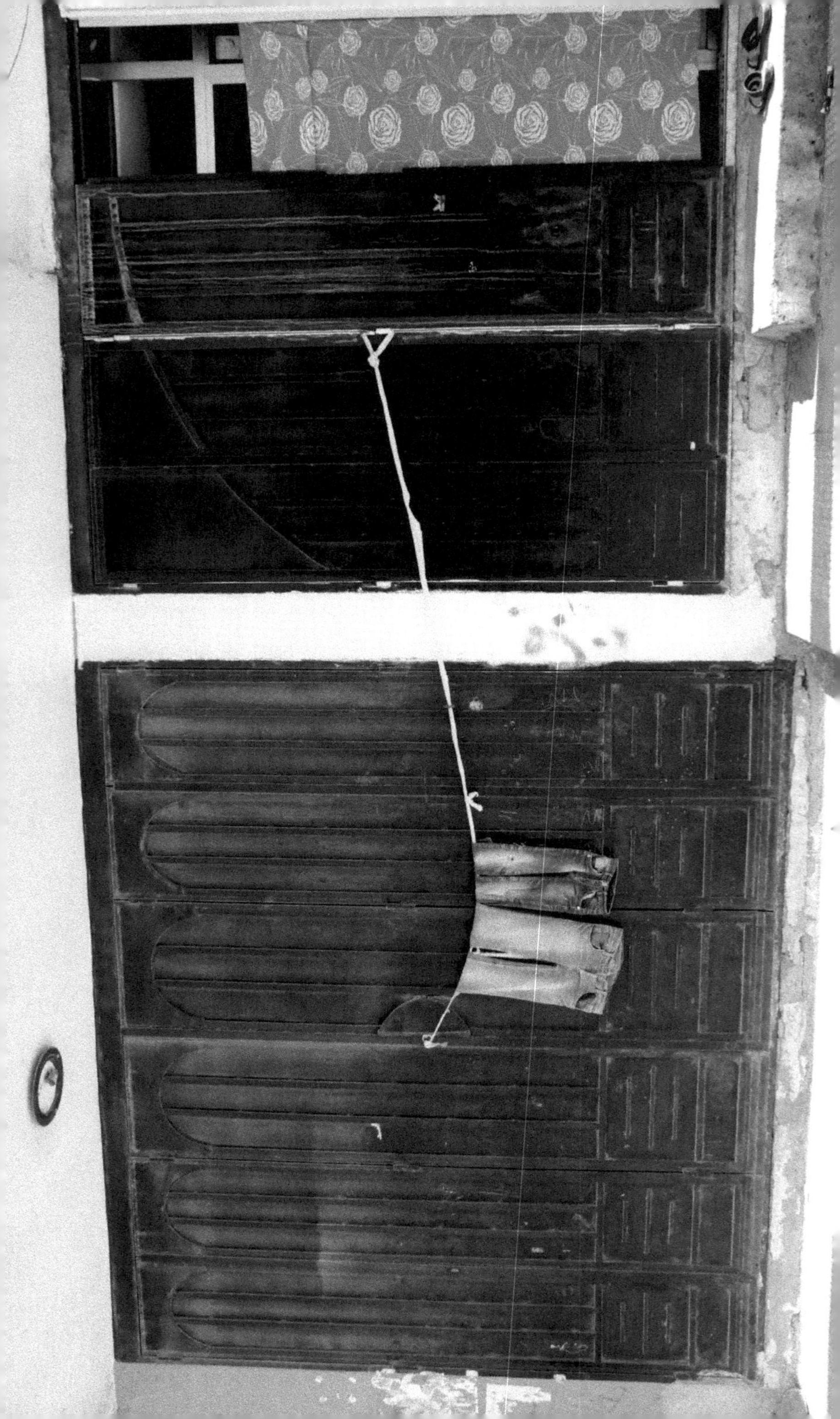

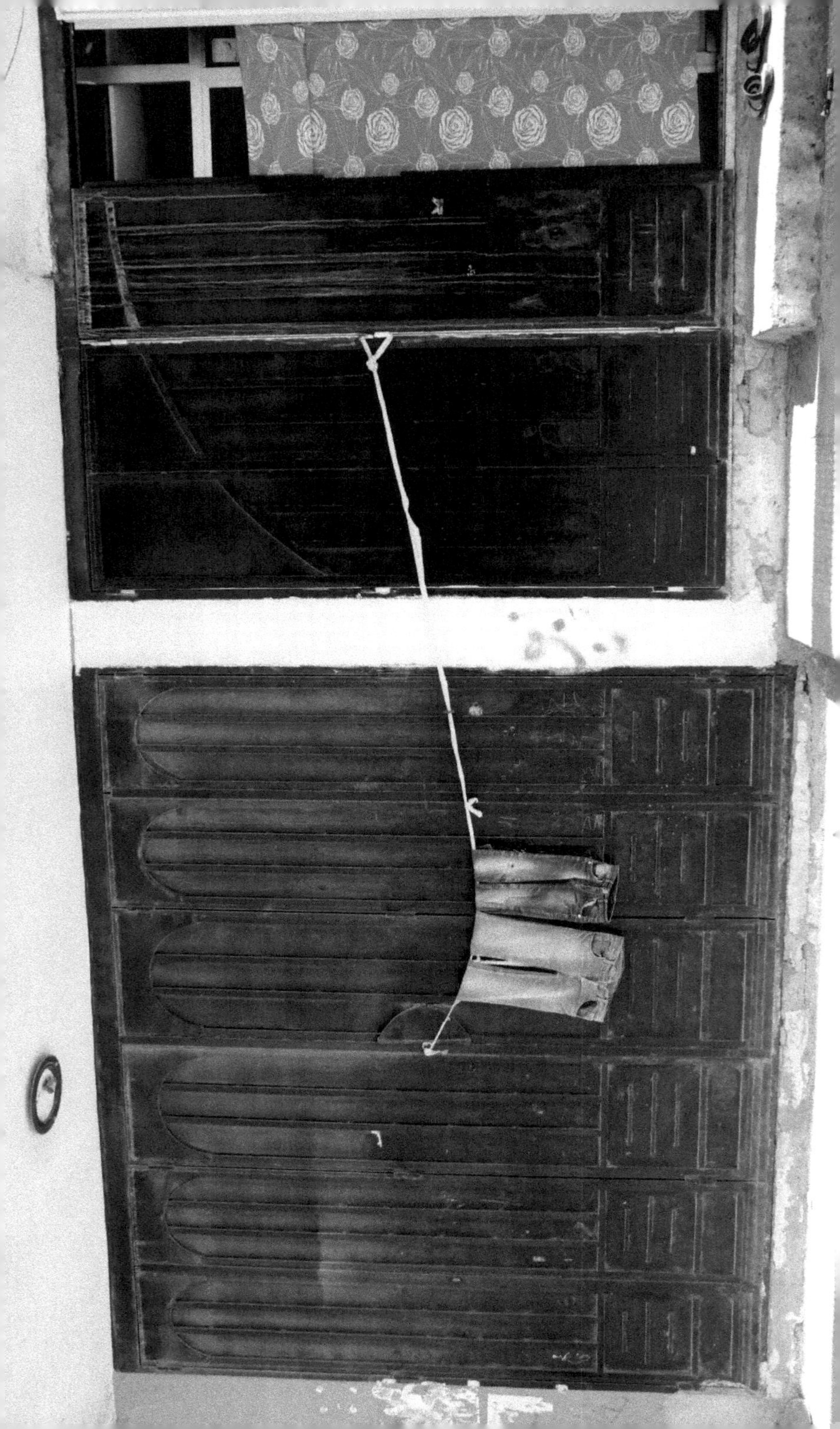

A DAILY RHYTHM INSIDE WHICH TIME CAN GROW...

Which is more intimate: the body in its absolute nakedness – concealed temporarily perhaps – or the nakedness in the thing, exposed or otherwise?

The place is a garage or a ground-floor room, a singular room with a small toilet, on the outskirts of Baddawi camp, occupied by some people, likely to be a young family, likely Syrian, likely present when the picture was taken.

But where were they exactly? What were they doing or not doing as the shutter induced the closure of the scene?

The weight of the two pairs of jeans, of different sizes, hung to dry against the black gate is palpable in the slight indentation or slope on the rope.

A red sheet, dotted with the outlines of white roses and leaves, guards the door – a sign of semi-normality and a marker of privacy to some extent.

A pair of slippers left obliquely on the threshold to separate, or so to claim the public from the private, hints at the presence of at least one person at the time.

The white wall, ceiling, and the makeshift washing-line, the black gates, the faded blue of the trousers, the red and white of the sheet, the brown-black slippers, the colours of things, people's things, stillness and life – colours which are being borne horizontally, vertically and sideways in an attempt to sustain a daily rhythm inside which time can grow.

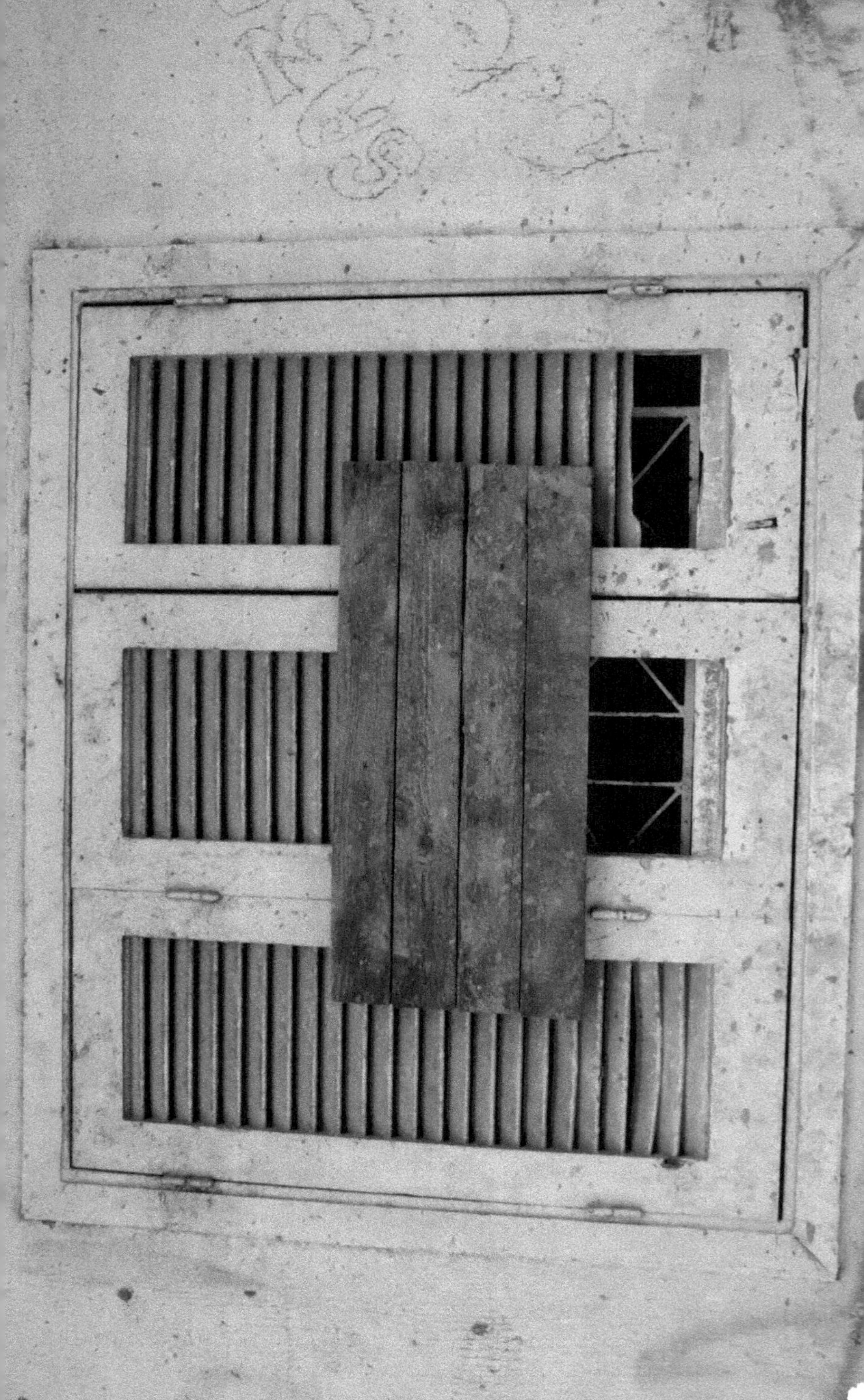

A WINDOW THROUGH WHICH THE SELF SEEPS

In its relentless retrieval of its time the photograph becomes. It becomes an occurrence as soon as it is seen as a separate time from what it is that it captures. Is it a window or the lateness of one that once was? The photograph does not offer an answer but suspends one. On the surface: a window's past shutters, grounding pieces of wood nailed across to support the fragile structure, to shut the window with firmness, reminding the seer that this is a place that still belongs to someone who is no longer there. But there is also the hole, or the two holes; the opening that exposes the metal work below the shutters, the extra texture that normally delays accessing the private that is inside. As if the eye sees itself in this inside darkness while it sees its way in and out by palpating different colours, segments, and tales. But what can an opening say? What can it narrate for the suspected absent? That its occurrence is subject to that of absence.

A Postscript:

Once it is open again, it will be heaven promising abundant time to those returning with the lightest of weights.

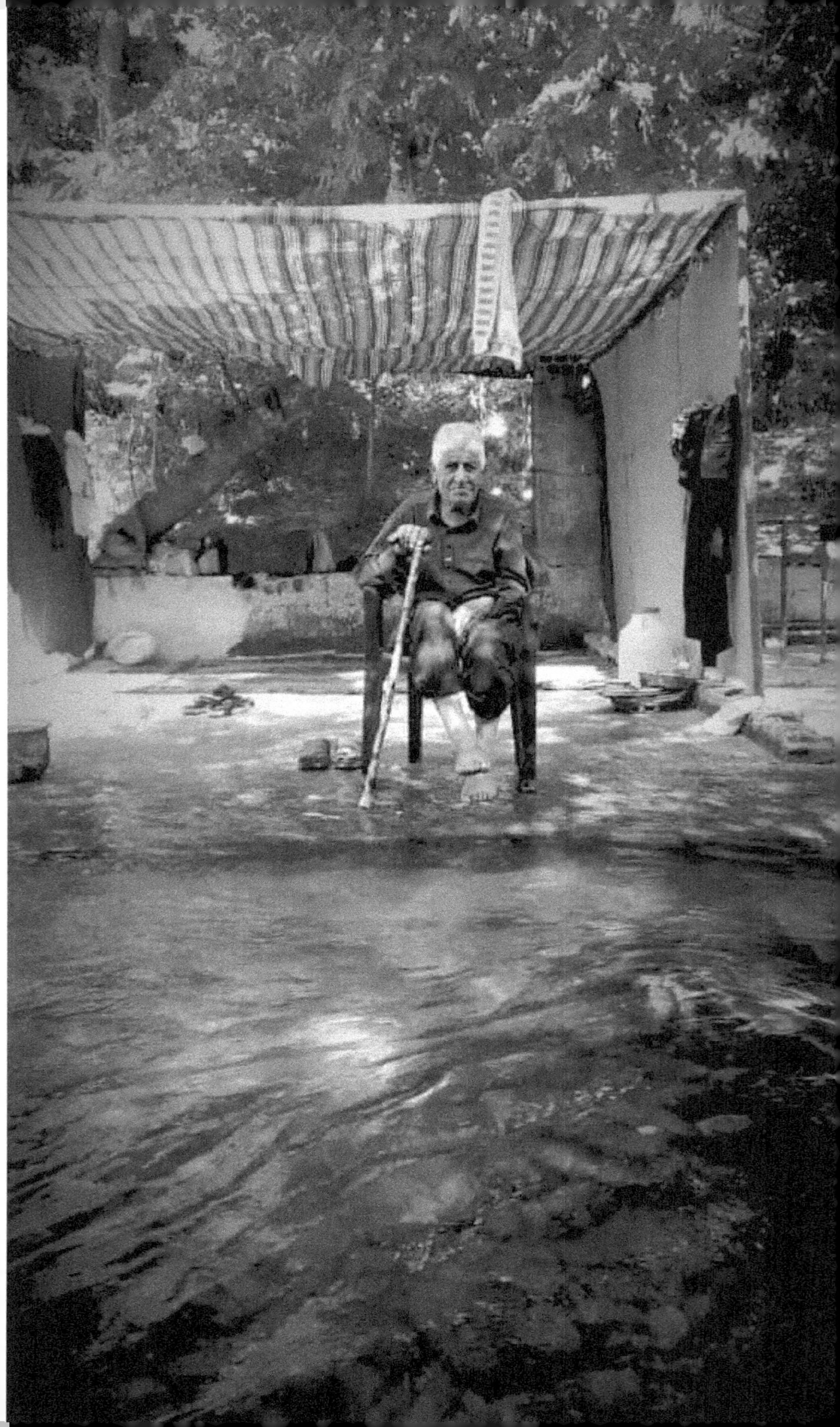

THERE WAS ONCE A VIEW

This is memory – or what remains of it.

The old man looks content with his surroundings, unintentionally breathing in as much air as he can in anticipation of a coming ruin. As if to say with the body opposite the lens: Inside what would become a photograph at a later time is a place for me and whoever comes after me, when neither I nor the place are anywhere to be seen. The feet are hovering over the ground, suspended exactly above the bank of a small creek passing by and minding its own course. Reaching the photograph, for the seer, means treading different terrains, many directions. On a plastic chair, he sits, like a diminutive god, the walking stick to the side to be grabbed when it is time for him to leave the frame. This might be another photograph but photographs, with time, can become anticipatory archives.

For a photograph from another place,

From a distant *bayt*, that is *home*, *tomb* and *verse*

□ □ □

The daughter cried, hair loose, hair tied: God! A dwelling is a fortune-teller's past.

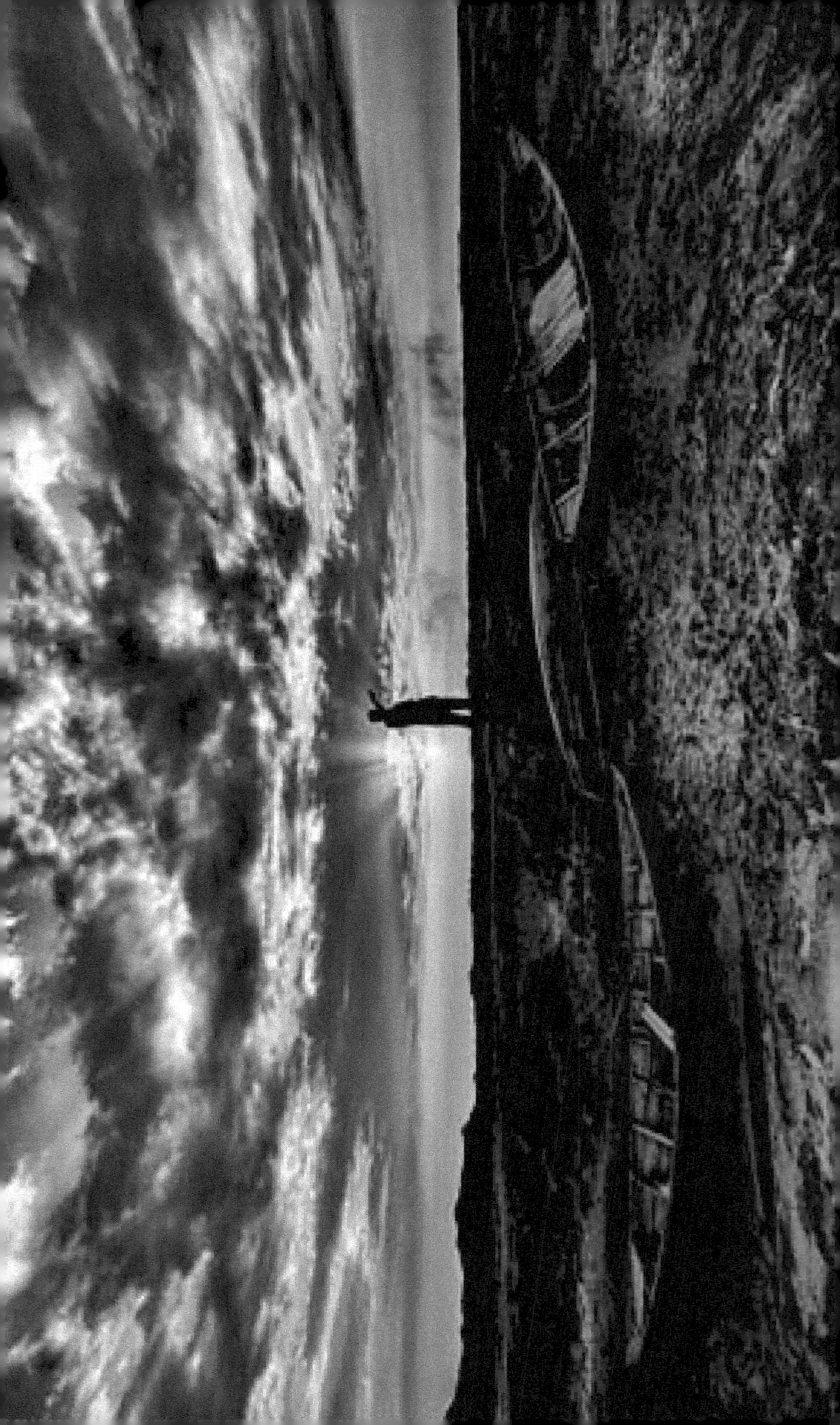

THE HUMAN THAT IS LACKING

Never to privilege seeing but to prod the blindness that is.

Co-seeing, if it were to happen, happens in the destruction that will be.

The seen, or what is presumed as such, has intact eyes but those who claim to see, and therefore have allegedly seen, have almost-eyes.

Apart from the silhouette and those who are not in the frame, the picture's center is inconspicuous. In black and white, at first glance, the picture appears trapped in the expansiveness of its stasis, easing the entrapment of all things scattered across its folds and their remains.

Everything inside the picture looks motionless, stranded: a silhouette pointing toward something. Toward a place, a thing, or people? To trace or guide those in the background? Or to feign movement, in a sighting where the human is visibly lacking and almost non-present.

Three fishing boats, elongated, two of almost similar length. The one in the middle, slightly shorter to the naked eye, is capsized, practically bridging the void between the other two boats. Those who may have boarded them appear out of the frame, but their footsteps, likely of bare feet, are still discernible in the undulated layers of mud. Could it be an arrival? A departure? Or could it be an unintended outing?

An arrival susceptible to its own arrival? A departure for an only alternative? Could those people, young, old, newborn, likely steeped in suppressed cries, have escaped a presence to seek another somewhere else? Textured mud, the clouds and one capacious cloud, punctured by an escaping ray of light, overshadowing all else and what digressionally can be seen as the inner. All alibis for an existence.

In pointing toward something—in all likelihood a thing that is known to those involved—space is, as it appears, divided into two unequal lots: what is in front of the outstretched arm and what is behind it or thereabouts. This thing of relevance that is definitely somewhere is exactly what the picture seems to allude to: the sense of sensing what may never be grasped and yet, for its sake, continues to live on in all things...

It is in the breathlessness detected in the loneliness of the pictured, that the picture outlives life, in so doing, becoming its own archive.

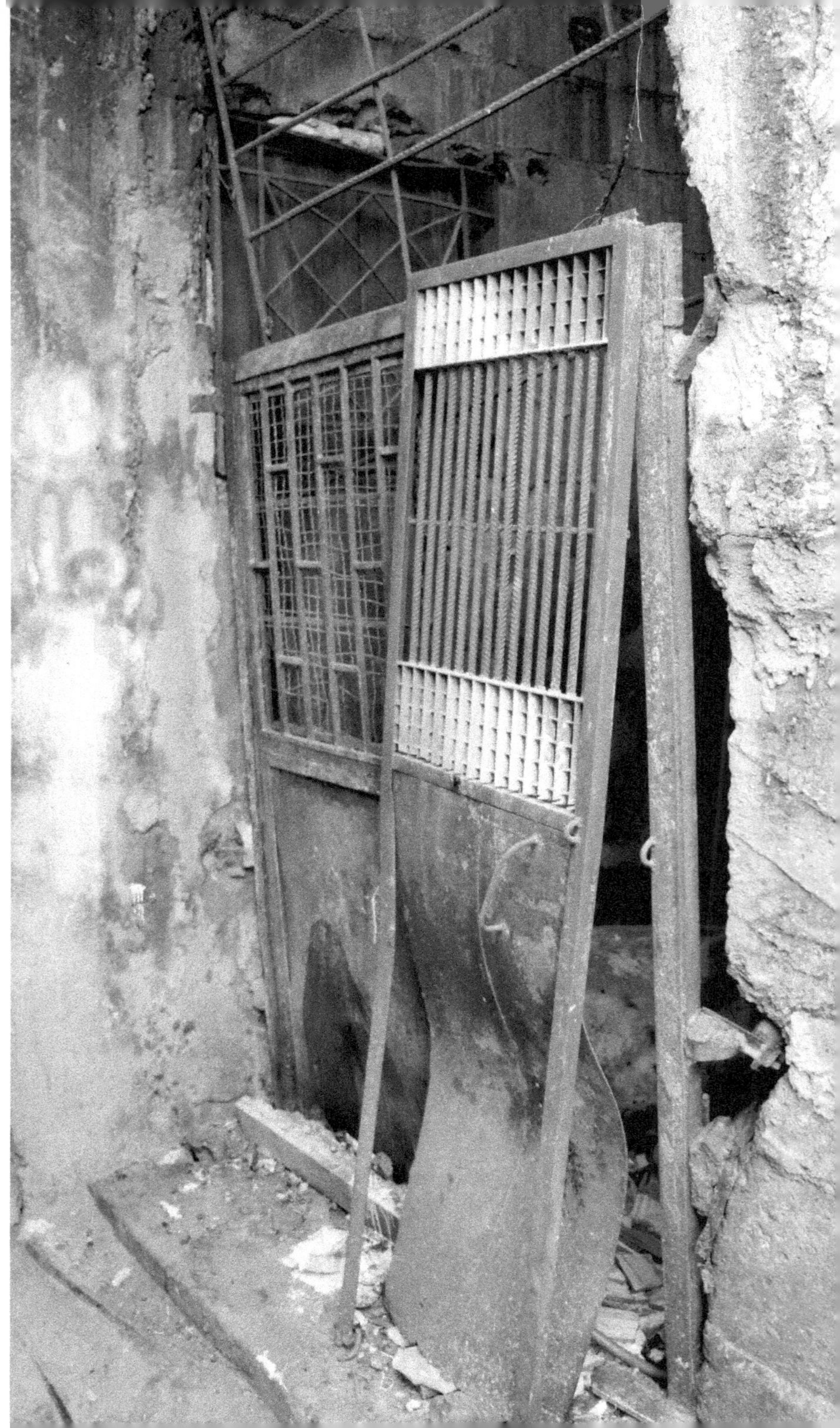

A GOD-CRAFTED DOOR

How is it possible for a metal door to inhere its past? It takes time. 'Time' is not the time that will be gathered post-event but rather the one contemplated as a response to the door's creation. The door's colour is the closest to its original colour – the colour which, as we were growing up in the camp, resembled a no-colour, simply that of the bomb shelter, a marker for entry and exit at the same time. I remember the interior as though it were now: darkness iterating another. I remember, for the love of dear life, clutching onto my mother's dress with every bang, benign or otherwise. I also remember standing at the bottom of the staircase wetting myself and sobbing, not wanting to be seen, not wanting my cries to be heard. My older sister's out-of-date chewing gum, the last four pieces as I recall, tucked in her trousers' pocket, would rattle as we carried our elderly neighbour's urine in a bucket to dispose of it, but fearing the light we would chuck it near our feet and run as fast as we could towards the darker darkness. Huddled together in one corner, my mother would remind us that soon all of this would be over.

When we were able to leave the shelter, we left behind three rotting bodies as a marker of a near return.

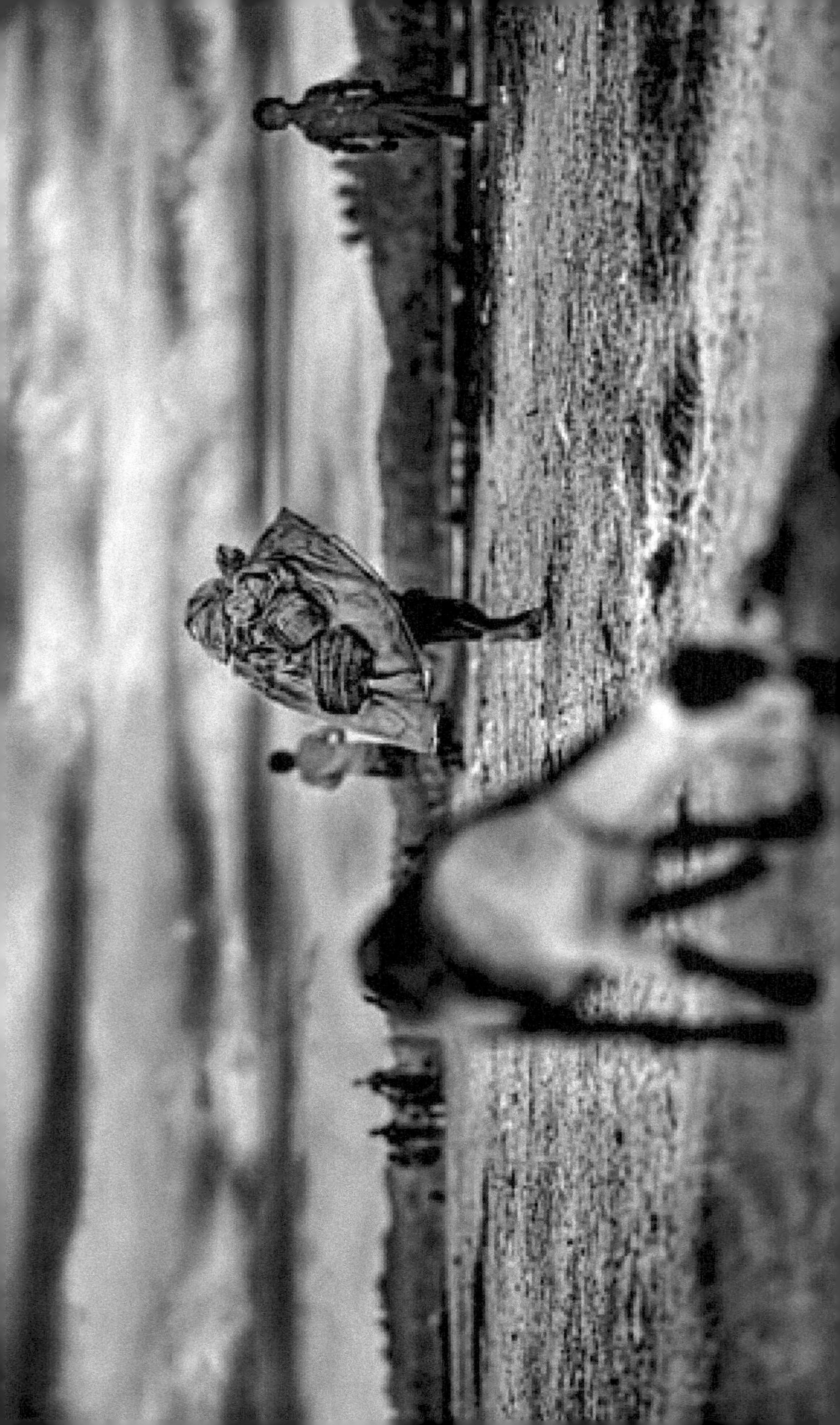

REMEMBERING IN PARTITIONS

I remember what we car-

ried: We bore to be borne. No slings

or cloth– Only flesh. Then, it was named the time, that

Time. The of-age hands bearing the brunt so

what's underneath is guarded in time. I carried the light then

the lightest. In single file, walking after the father, not stepping on

his foot, not rocking the boat. For every stride, is a life waiting.
The living who remember

in partitions so home is an accumulation of things – a bag darned

in daylight. *Hurry!* He shouted. *This is the first load.*

From shoulder to shoulder, he tentatively balanced the weight.
Eyes squinting as though

nothing had survived the eyes. To outlive our shadows, we carried
the already dead.

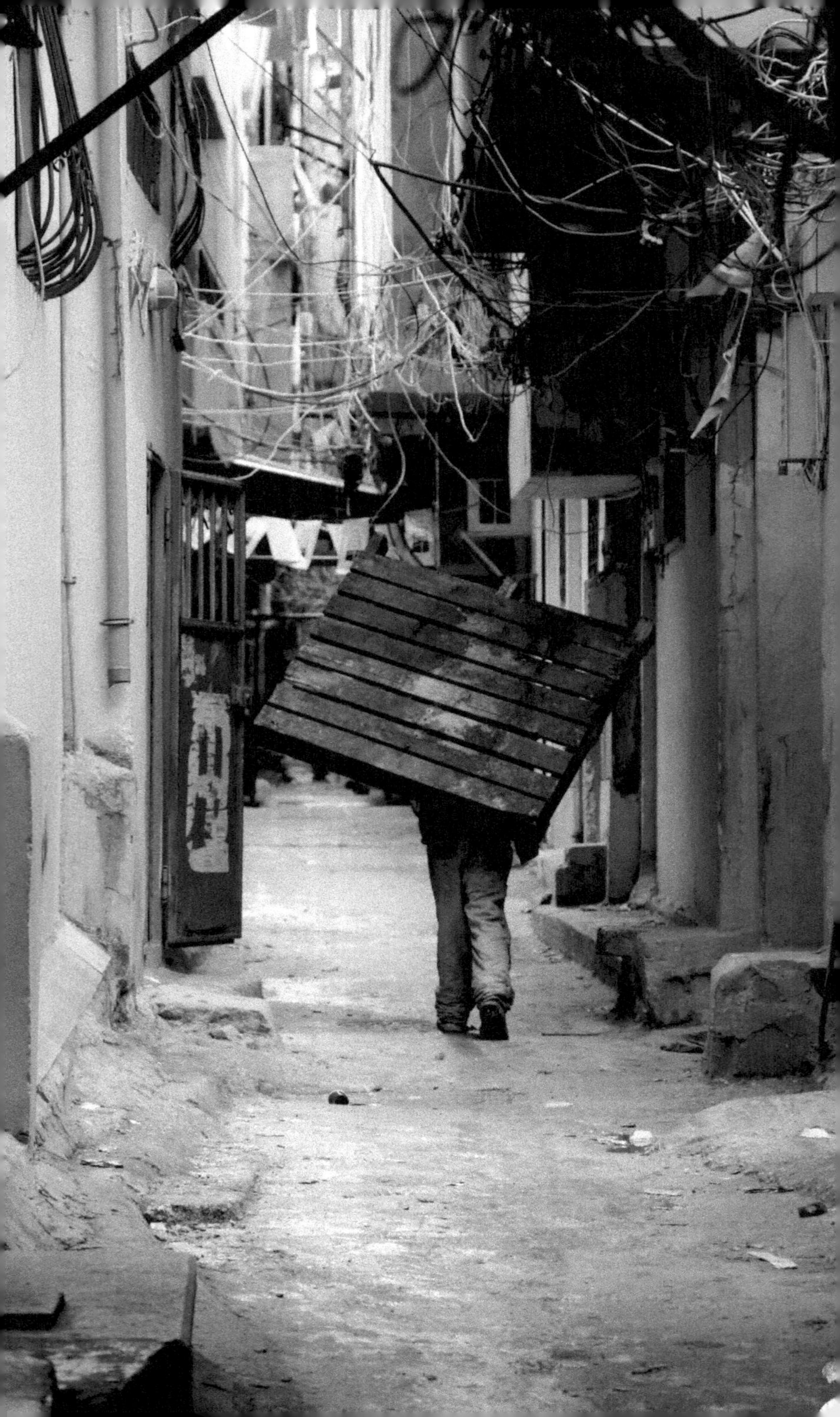

ON THE WAY TO THE ALTAR

Burdens are continuous.

As we bear them, they bear us. In a way, we swap hands with them, without relinquishing our bodies.

It is the truth that the body is a burden. This is the refugee body carrying itself to the altar. Not awaiting ceremonies or wakes.

... from damp wood and beads we made a crucifix.

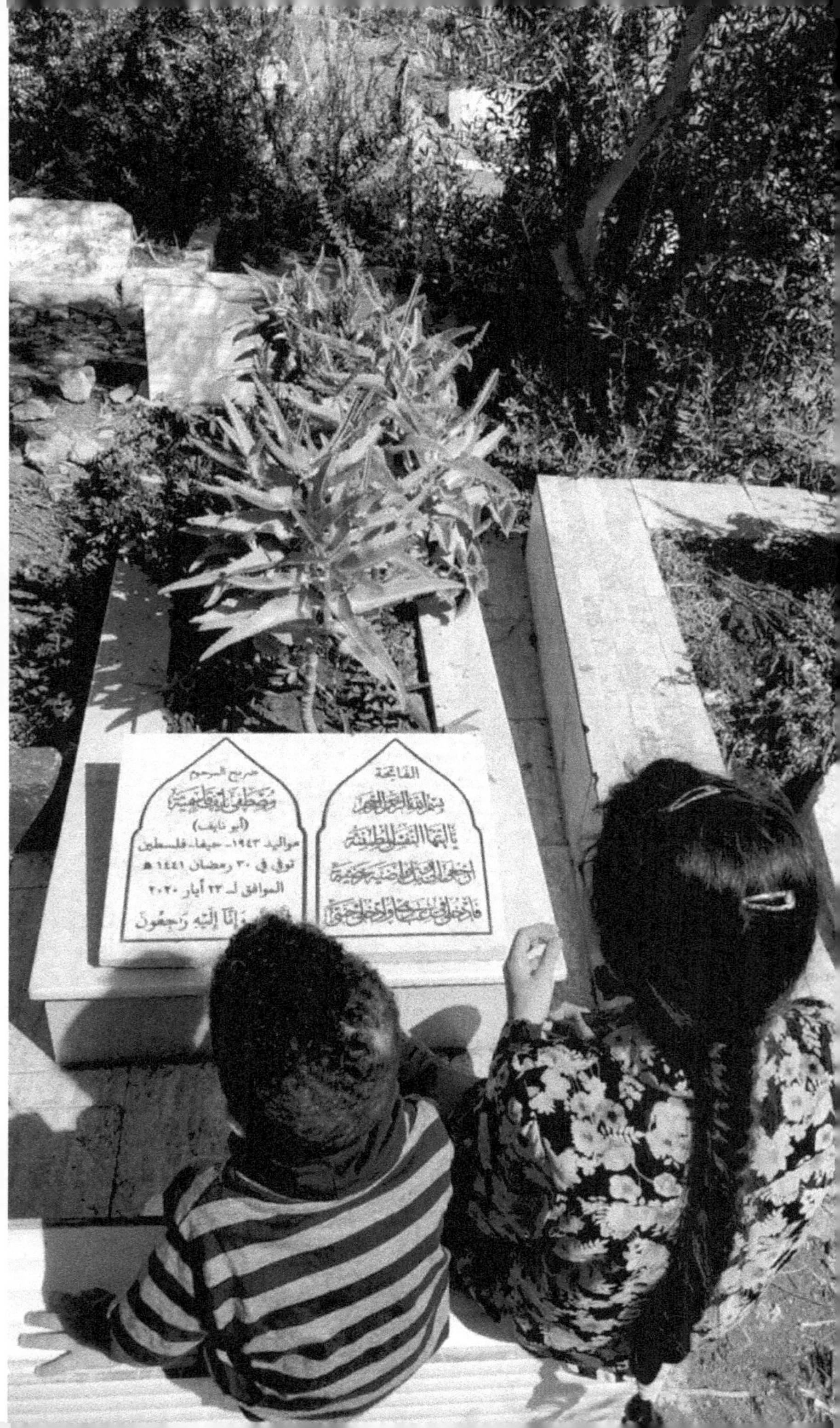

الفاتحة
بسم الله الرحمن الرحيم
يا أيتها النفس المطمئنة
ارجعي إلى ربك راضية مرضية
فادخلي في عبادي وادخلي جنتي
ضريح المرحوم
(أبو نايف)
مواليد ١٩٤٣ - حيفا - فلسطين
توفي في ٣٠ رمضان ١٤٤١ هـ
الموافق لـ ٢٣ أيار ٢٠٢٠
إنا إليه راجعون

THE TOMB IS A FURROW

For the dead to sense the living, there should be a common ground. That common ground is the dialect that rests at the threshold of *Fusha* as the dead and the living merge into one in their own words. So it is the *Fatiha* that is being read over the dead's head, *the Opening*, in English, that cuts through the decreed silence of God until it reaches the dead, as another, in their afterlife. What a journey?! And for it to be a journey there should be the pending return to the meaning of the photographed in full. I recite the *Fatiha* as well, in the background lamenting my father's eyes and smell. I remind myself that it must not be permanent and that death is just for a while – a short while – but that is not true and that death is the truth since it is both seen and felt. It is the back of the tomb's visitor that is captured, so the face is solely granted to the dead and so the other cannot detract from their other in death. I water the tomb. Water purchased in gallons. Water extracted from the soil so it returns to it in abundance and verity.

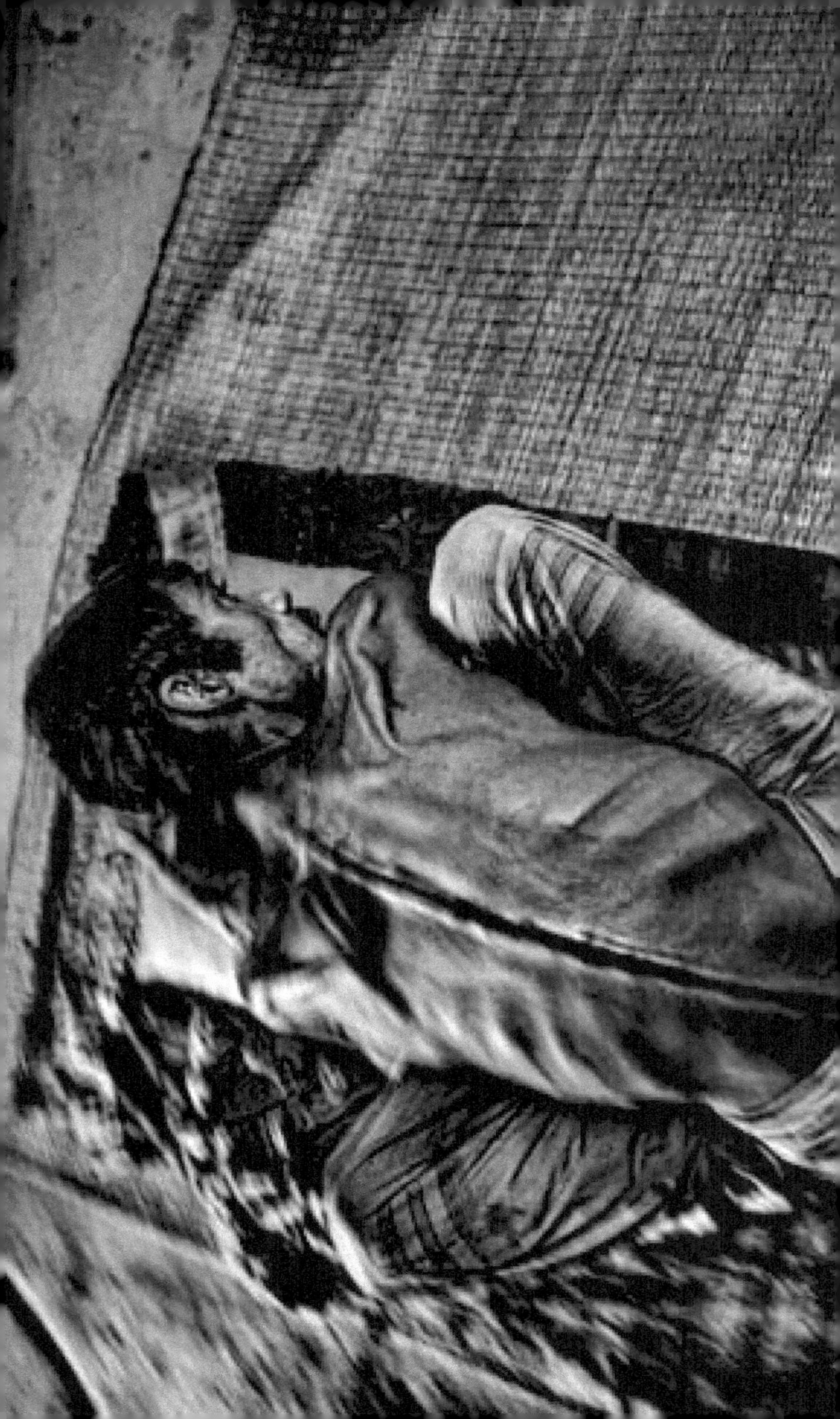

THE BODY IN PAIN

Bodies are different, not only as bodies but as subsequent interpretations on their own. In the photograph, the body is in the open. It is that of an ill and neglected subject, caught between visibility and its opposite borne in the black and white, rendering the human back, in its protruding bones and scars, a mound – or a last shrine for the impatient onlookers. The body in this case substitutes its bearer, it strips him of his autonomy so it is reshaped as a second body, both subject to seeing and yet in charge of what is out there in the first place to be seen. Seized on a mat, even two, the photograph closes in the body from above where nakedness, or total exposure, seems to be elevated above the rest of the body and where the covered part is on the cusp of splitting apart and dissolving. This time the face does not completely depart. It stays in the vicinity despite its disappearing eyes, beholding its happening while belonging in a new time.

Even if the name, bestowed from above, is for the body, and the named is that body, the seen will always be that of the unseen.

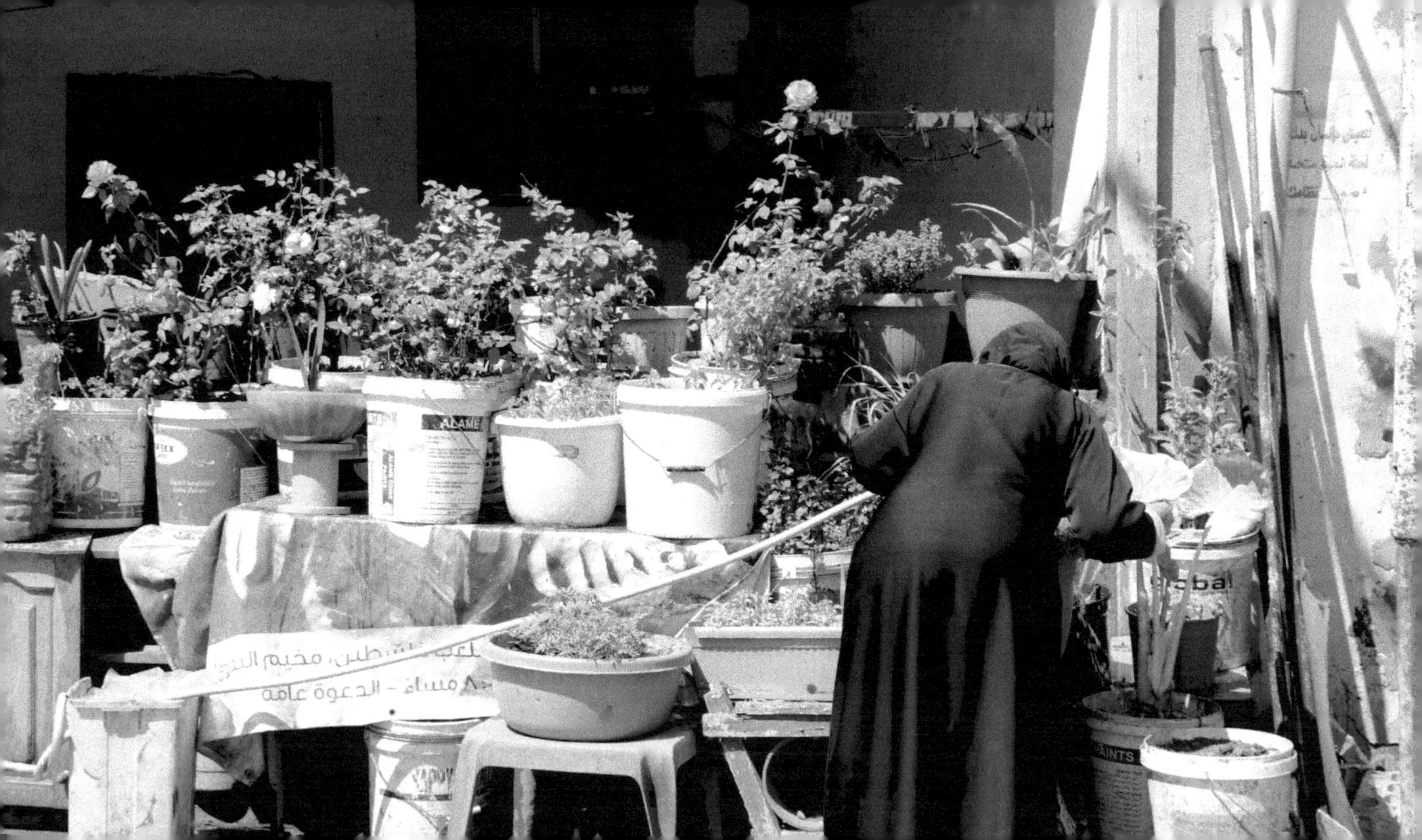
الدعوة عامة
PAINTS

TO THE PLANTS IS HER FACE

The plants which appear in this picture hinge partly on a short wall and partly on a used wooden chest of drawers primarily staged to encircle the entrance to the house and protect it from the curious eyes of passers-by. Or to 'privatise' part of the public space by appropriating it.

Underneath some of the pots, to the woman's left, a recycled banner made of fabric, likely nylon, from a previous event that still bears the Arabic: ... Palestine, Baddawi Camp, 8pm, All Welcome.

It is clear that the woman tending to the plants is the owner of the house. She waters the plants through a yellow hose that enables her to reach the other end without substantially altering her position.

Dressed in kohl-like blue, contrasted with a headscarf of a lighter shade of blue, she leans towards the first row of plants with her back to the main road.

She looks engrossed in what she is doing, with her right hand almost touching a pale leaf – perhaps to snap it off its mother plant.

The non-ordinariness of this scene does not lie in the co-presence between the canonical grey of the camp and the green exception, but precisely in its interruptive nature as an anomaly whose sole value is to overpower the norm in/of the camp to make it more visible and 'normal'.

It is the "beauty" "at the expense" and never "in conjunction with" or "in accordance to" that matters in this photograph – a photograph whose meaning is that of the place.

POSTSCRIPT

How is displacement conceptualised and represented when viewed and written from the perspective of the refugee camp, the host city, the border? The photographs and writings in the preceding pages are born of a collaboration which is both South-South and Displacement-to-Displacement, embracing the works of the Palestinian poet, Yousif M. Qasmiyeh and Bangladeshi photographer, Saiful Huq Omi, together with members of the Baddawi Camp community, who have taken and shared photographs and reflections of and since their home-camp.

Through bringing their poetry and photography into conversation with one another, not in search of congruence or comparison, but of echoes and resemblances, this book explores the nature and potentialities of Southern and South-South representations of displacement, examining how refugees and artists respond both to 'their own' displacement situations, and also to the displacement of 'others'.

With a focus on photography and poetry produced and co-produced in relation to Baddawi refugee camp in Lebanon (established in the 1950s to provide shelter to Palestinian refugees, and hosting refugees from Syria — including Syrians, Palestinian Syrians, Iraqis and Kurds — since 2011) and Bangladesh (which has been hosting Rohingya refugees since the 1970s, including in Cox's Bazaar and in Dhaka), we plant a seed and an intention: to engage meaningfully with the question of *self*-archiving displacement in photography and writing, and also to explore the potentialities of *co-seeing and co-writing* displacements of the self and other through an explicitly relational, South-South process.

ACKNOWLEDGEMENTS

This book is the outcome of a series of intersecting and ongoing conversations, collaborations and projects. These include, but are not limited to: the Baddawi Camp Research Lab (led by Yousif M. Qasmiyeh and Elena Fiddian-Qasmiyeh as part of the AHRC-funded Imagining Futures research programme directed and overseen by Elena Isayev, to whom we are so grateful); *Analysing South-South Humanitarian Responses to Displacement from Syria: Views from Lebanon, Jordan and Turkey* (funded by the European Research Council under the Horizon 2020 Research and Innovation agreement no. 715582); *Refugee Hosts* (funded by the AHRC-ESRC under grant number AH/P005438/1); initiatives supported by the UKRI-GCRF and UCL's GCRF and Newton Consolidation Accounts; and ongoing research funded by the Philip Leverhulme Prize (PLP-2015-250), all led by Elena Fiddian-Qasmiyeh.

The following pieces by Yousif M. Qasmiyeh and the accompanying photographs by Elena Fiddian-Qasmiyeh were originally published as part of the Refugee Hosts research project: 'There will always be a vendor before and after the picture'; 'A daily rhythm inside which time can grow'; 'The Hands are Hers'; and 'To the Plants is her Face'. An earlier version of the photograph and reflection titled 'A God-crafted Door' was originally commissioned and published as part of the Imagining Futures research programme under the original title 'The Bomb Shelter.' 'The Human that Is Lacking' was first published in *Migration and Society*, 4 (2021): 201–202.

The photographs by Saiful Huq Omi were originally published in his 2018 book *136: I am Rohingya* (Schilt Publishing).

We are hugely indebted to all of the residents of Baddawi Camp who contributed to the initiatives underpinning this book by sharing their memories and family photographs with us, some of which are included in these pages. We extend our special thanks in particular to Ahmad Basal, Ahmad Obeid, Aliyyah Qaddoura, Ata Mustafa Qasmiyeh, Ayman Al-Sayyed, Bilal Al-Sayyed, Eman Mohammed Ghannam, Imad Al-Sayyed, Imad Suleiyman Al-Hasan, Inas Al-Sayyed, Mahmoud Mustafa Qasmiyeh, Maysoun Mustafa, Nahlah Al-Khalid (Imm Ahmad) Basal, Taha Al-Aasi, and Tariq Al-Sayyed. Beyond these specific names, our profound thanks go to the extended families in the camp and on its outskirts who have welcomed us and have made the book itself possible.

Our most heartfelt thanks to Aaron Kent and Broken Sleep Books for believing in and supporting this book from the outset.

CREDITS

p. 10 Image by Saiful Huq Omi (_MG_2121, from *136: I am Rohingya,* Schilt Publishing)

p. 12 Image by Elena Fiddian-Qasmiyeh

p. 14 Image by Saiful Huq Omi (_MG_5822, from *136: I am Rohingya,* Schilt Publishing)

p. 16 Family archive of Ahmad Obeid and Imad Suleiyman Al-Hasan

p. 18 Image by Elena Fiddian-Qasmiyeh

p. 20 Image by Saiful Huq Omi (IMG_6589, from *136: I am Rohingya,* Schilt Publishing)

p. 22 Family archive of Nahlah Al-Khalid (Imm Ahmad) Basal

p. 24 Image by Saiful Huq Omi (_MG_6811, from *136: I am Rohingya,* Schilt Publishing)

p. 26 Image by Elena Fiddian-Qasmiyeh

p. 28 Image by Saiful Huq Omi (702A3983.jpg, from *136: I am Rohingya,* Schilt Publishing)

p. 30 Family archive of Imad Al-Sayyed and Aliyyah Qaddoura

p. 32 Image by Elena Fiddian-Qasmiyeh

p. 34 Image by Elena Fiddian-Qasmiyeh

p. 36 Family archive of Nahlah Al-Khalid (Imm Ahmad) Basal

p. 38 Image by Saiful Huq Omi (IMG_7855, from *136: I am Rohingya,* Schilt Publishing)

p. 42 Image by Elena Fiddian-Qasmiyeh

p. 44 Image by Saiful Huq Omi (_MG_1905, from *136: I am Rohingya,* Schilt Publishing)

p. 46 Image by Elena Fiddian-Qasmiyeh

p. 48 Family archive of Ata Mustafa Qasmiyeh

p. 50 Image by Saiful Huq Omi (IMG_6668, from *136: I am Rohingya,* Schilt Publishing)

p. 52 Image by Elena Fiddian-Qasmiyeh

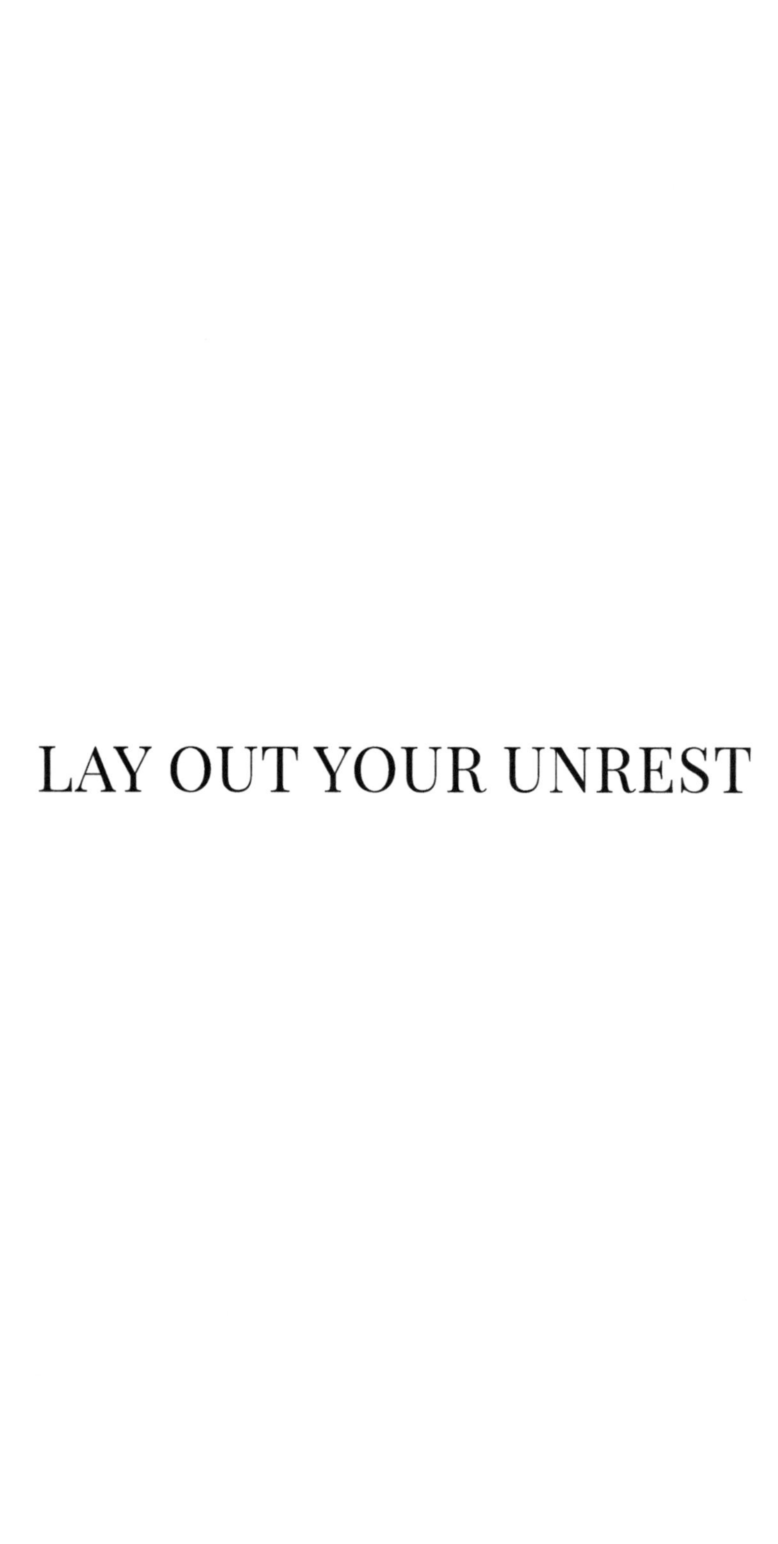

LAY OUT YOUR UNREST

www.ingramcontent.com/pod-product-compliance
Lightning Source LLC
LaVergne TN
LVHW052343100826
845147LV00021B/1168

9781916938427

PHOTOGRAPHY FROM OVER THERE – WHY?

Since birth, the impulse to stake claims in time and place is there. Because photographs are transferrable memories and objects, their travelling is also the travelling of us, refugees and citizens. The photographs we take and those taken of us, at times unawares, are all belongings in lieu of other belongings. While they remain within themselves, they are equally shared as extended items: See and be seen. Carry and be carried. Remember and be remembered. That is why photographs linger at the edge of things and people so much so that they swap places with them.

Look, who's there?

Look, who was there?

Whoever is in the photograph is a god despite their undivine nature. Why? Because within the parameters of the photograph they create themselves as creators, not creatures, of the archive – as self-creators. As auto-photographers even when such photographs are not taken by them. It is their archive after all. The space in which their existence dwells. The time that never fails to return to them.

Undoubtedly it is an enviable privilege to keep photographs, more so to take them, since what is kept is kept for the future and not everyone is granted the same access to the future. Most refugees in this book document for themselves before the future. I remember my father disembowelling bits of Sellotape, turning them inside out, to stick our photographs in the family album, tenderly balancing the weight of each photograph as he would fix